Prehistory and Protohistory of India

— An Appraisal —

(Palaeolithic — Non-Harappan Chalcolithic Cultures)

Perspectives in Indian Art & Archaeology
ISSN 0971-4723

1. **The Splendour of Mathurā Art and Museum**; by R.C. Sharma; ISBN 978-81-246-0015-3

2. **Proto-Historic Pottery of Indus Valley Civilisation** : Study of Painted Motif; by Sudha Satyawadi; ISBN 978-81-246-0030-6

3. **Saptamātòkā Worship and Sculptures** : An Iconological Interpretation of Conflicts and Resolutions in the Storied Brāhmanical Icons; by Shivaji K. Panikkar; ISBN 978-81-246-0074-0

4. **Elements of Indian Art** : Including Temple Architecture, Iconography & Iconometry; by S.P. Gupta and Shashi Prabha Asthana; ISBN 978-81-246-0213-3 (Hb); ISBN 978-81-246-0214-0 (Pb)

5. **Bull in Early Indian Art** : Up to Sixth Century AD; by Bhogendra Jha; ISBN 978-81-246-0255-3

6. **Bibliography on Indian Buddhist Art and Archaeology** : General and Classified under Geographical Sites; by Utpal Chakraborty; ISBN 978-81-246-0361-1

8-9. **Śiva-Pārvatī and Allied Images** : Their Iconography and Body Language; by Thomas Eugene Donaldson; ISBN 978-81-246-0359-8

10. **Temples in India** : Origin and Developmental Stages; by S.P. Gupta and S. Vijayakumar; ISBN 978-81-246-0495-3 (Hb); ISBN 978-81-246-0496-0 (Pb)

11. **The Power of the Female** : Devāṅganā Sculptures on Indian Temple Architecture; by Gauri Parimoo Krishnan; ISBN 978-81-246-0687-2

12. **Gods, Men and Women** : Gender and Sexuality in Early Indian Art; by Seema Bawa; ISBN 978-81-246-0664-3

Perspectives in Indian Art & Archaeology, no. 7

Prehistory and Protohistory of India

— An Appraisal —

Palaeolithic — Non-Harappan Chalcolithic Cultures

V.K. Jain

Foreword by

Professor D.N. Jha

PRINTWORLD

Publishers of Indian Traditions

Cataloging in Publication Data — DK

[Courtesy: D.K. Agencies (P) Ltd. <docinfo@dkagencies.com>]

Jain, V.K. (Vardhman Kumar), author.
Prehistory and protohistory of India : an appraisal : palaeolithic, non-Harappan Chalcolithic cultures / V.K. Jain ; foreword by Professor D.N. Jha.
pages cm. – (Perspectives in Indian art & archaeology, ISSN 0971-4723 ; no. 7)
Reprint. Originally published: 2006.
Includes bibliographical references and index.
ISBN 9788124603727 (HB)
ISBN 9788124603734 (PB)

1. India – Antiquities. 2. India – Civilization – To 1200. 3. Prehistoric peoples – India. 4. Protohistory. I. Title. II. Series : Perspectives in Indian art & archaeology ; no. 7.

LCC DS418.J35 2025 | DDC 934 23

ISBN 978-81-246-0372-7 (Hardbound)
ISBN 978-81-246-0373-4 (Paperback)
First Published in India in 2006
Reprinted in 2009, 2014, 2015, 2017, 2018, 2020, 2021 and 2025

Printed and published by:
D.K. Printworld (P) Ltd.
Regd. Office: "Vedaśrī", F-395, Sudarshan Park
ESI Hospital Metro Station, New Delhi - 110015
Phones: (011) 4172 2626, 98713 94815
e-mail: indology@dkprintworld.com
Website: www.dkprintworld.com

Dedicated
as a token of respect and gratitude
to
Professor R.S. Sharma

Foreword

MUCH work has been done in the field of Indian archaeology during the last fifty years or so as is evident from the large number of explorations and excavations that have been undertaken during this period and from the vast amount of literature that has been generated by archaeologists. Although many excavation reports have remained unpublished, scholars have made good use of whatever material is available in print and have deepened our understanding of India's past. The information and interpretation contained in the archaeological literature, however, have yet to find their due place in the textbooks and become accessible to teachers as well as students. The present work by Dr. V.K. Jain is a commendable effort in this direction.

An inspiring teacher of long standing and a dedicated researcher, Dr. V.K. Jain has painstakingly rummaged through the entire relevant literature and has ably tried to assimilate the available data. Unswayed by any trendy and fashionable approach he has dealt with controversial issues in a highly detached manner and has presented a comprehensive view of the latest information on tools and technologies, subsistence patterns, and distribution and ecological background of settlements during the period from the Palaeolithic to the non-Harappan Chalcolithic. The appendix on the megalithic cultures of Central India and the Deccan, the line drawings of tools, and the explanatory notes on important archaeological sites accompanied by maps are some of the important features of the book which make it extremely useful for the readers. I am sure the students as well as teachers will find Dr. Jain's book an indispensable handbook on Indian prehistory and protohistory and will eagerly wait for the publication of its companion volume on the Harappan culture.

D.N. Jha
Former Professor of History
University of Delhi

Preface

FRESH excavations, new dating techniques and ever-growing conceptual frameworks during the last half-a-century have greatly reshaped our perspective on Prehistoric and Protohistoric past of the Indian subcontinent. But still most of the books and articles on the subject, with the exception of those by D.K. Chakrabarti, F.R. Allchin, D.P. Agarwal, K. Paddayya and a few others, continue to follow the traditional "culture-history" paradigm or collection and narration approach rather than focus on the cultural process of change and continuity. Since 1950, the pace of research has increased manifold and there is today enough data to portray more or less a clear and connected picture of India's cultural growth in the remote past, and to justify the argument that there is nothing 'static' about Indian society which, as any other, has been growing with time and space.

This monograph is an attempt to present, in a concise but comprehensive manner, a syncretic view of the latest information on tools and technologies, settlement-subsistence pattern, distributional framework and ecological background, etc., in respect of Prehistory and Protohistory of India. It covers a canvas extending from the Palaeolithic to the non-Harappan Chalcolithic Cultures and leaves out the Harappan Civilization for the subsequent volume. It begins with an enquiry into the definition of Prehistory and Protohistory and goes on to refer to the significance of latest dating techniques and theoretical perspectives in archaeology. Chapter-II reviews the contribution which Indian archaeological studies since 1950 have made to our knowledge. In the subsequent chapters, the salient features of Palaeolithic, Mesolithic, Neolithic and non-Harappan Chalcolithic Cultures have been highlighted. The chief elements of the iron-using Megalithic Cultures of peninsular India and the Deccan (c. 1000 BC – 300 BC), the information about which is obtained exclusively from the archaeological excavations, have been discussed in the Appendix which also includes a glossary of important terms frequently used in archaeological as well as the explanatory notes on prominent sites mentioned in the text.

This book is an enlarged version of the chapters initially intended for inclusion in an advanced level text-book by a multi-scholar team and, therefore, it naturally has a student oriented format though a general reader who is inquisitive enough to know more about India's remotest past may also find it beneficial. The biggest difficulty in writing a text of this nature lies in deciding what to include and what to exclude. And for this I have taken the liberty of using my academic experience and discretion because in a subject which is so full of details and unresolved issues and controversies, it is just not possible to do justice to each and every fact or interpretation. It has been my endeavour to draw a compromise between the extremes of technicality and generality, and confine more to highlighting the important features of cultural growth. Archaeological jargons have been kept to the minimum and, whenever used, they have been fully explained in the text or in the glossary at the end. For the purpose of conveying the visual interpretation, line-drawings, illustrations and maps have been included, wherever required. For a reader who is stimulated enough to know more, a select bibliography is appended to the text.

Some repetition and errors of facts or spellings may no doubt remain. The author will be delighted to receive from anyone the suggestions for corrections or improvements.

I shall like to place on record my gratitude to all those scholars whose contributions have been utilized fruitfully in writing this book.

I also wish to gratefully acknowledge the support and encouragement that I received from Prof. B.P. Sahu, Head, Department of History, Delhi University and Prof. R.C. Thakran, also of the Delhi University. I am thankful to many of my friends and well-wishers at the National Museum, the Archaeological Survey of India and the Motilal Nehru College for their help in many ways. My thanks are due to Shri D.P. Sharma, In-Charge Prehistory Section at the National Museum, Delhi for readily helping with the books, articles and suggestions whenever needed. I am grateful to Dr. Nagarch, formerly Director of the Archaeological Survey of India, for going through the proofs and making valuable comments.

I am thankful to the library staff of the Archaeological Survey of India and the National Museum, particularly Shri Bhagwan Chaube, for providing me with all possible assistance in procuring the material necessary for writing the book.

I am highly indebted to Prof. D.N. Jha, a scholar of international repute and the General President of the Indian History Congress (66th session, Santiniketan), who, in spite of a very busy schedule and numerous obligations, has been kind enough to oblige me with a foreword for this book.

I shall like to record my great sense of appreciation for the personal interest which Shri Susheel Mittal of the D.K. Printworld (P) Ltd. took in bringing about the book in a record time.

Last but not the least, my thanks go to my wife Dr. Krishna Jain and my son Siddharth for supporting me all through this task of preparing the manuscript with love, patience and good humour.

I take the privilege of dedicating this book, as a token of regard and gratitude, to Prof. R.S. Sharma who has throughout been devoted to the task of promoting secular and scientific approach in Indological studies. As the founder-Chairman of the Indian Council of Historical Research, New Delhi, he was instrumental in giving a positive direction to historical studies, whereas at the University of Delhi, where he was a Professor and the Head of the Department of History in 1970s, he had generated among students a new sense of enthusiasm and encouragement for research on various aspects of social and economic history. Those of us who have been associated with him, either as a student or a researcher, can never forget his kindness, grace and commitment to the subject.

Contents

List of Maps and Figures

1

Introduction

What is Prehistory?

PREHISTORY refers to that phase of human history when earth was still taking shape and man was evolving biologically through various extinct species from the primates to its present form. It is a history of early man's struggle for survival in adverse environment and is marked by his steady progress from an animal-hunting and wild food-collecting wandering life to that of a food-producing and cattle-herding settled life.

Since early human did not know writing, his artifacts, i.e. the things which are deliberately fashioned by him to meet his needs and requirements, such as tools of stone, bone or any other material, pottery, pieces of ornaments, etc. form the only source which stand mute witness to his cultural and material progress. Besides these, the traces of huts, hearths, querns and burials too help us in gaining information on the life-pattern and thought-process of the early humans. During the last half a century, the fresh excavations and new dating techniques along with growing multi-disciplinary approach have not only greatly added to our knowledge but have also changed our perspective and understanding of Prehistory. Today, the Prehistoric tools and artifacts are treated not an end but as the means to understand early human's endeavour to feed and protect himself in adverse climatic conditions.

In archaeological terminology, there are, besides "Prehistory," two other phases in which human civilization is divided, and these are termed as "Protohistory" and "History." Protohistory is a period when man had become literate but on account of our inability to decipher his records, as in the case of the Harappan Civilization, the data derived from the discovered material objects remains unsupplemented, and our information on his life pattern continues to be hazy and incomplete. Protohistory is also treated as a phase that bridges the gulf between c. 3000 BC and 600 BC. The period referred to as "History," on the other hand, is the one when we come across ample records in the form of literary texts and epigraphs which help us to cross-examine the data and help us in reinforcing our knowledge on human history with greater precision.

Chronologically, Prehistory covers the largest period of human history. Since stone was the chief material that was used by early man to procure food or to protect himself, this period is also described as the Stone Age. In Europe the study of Prehistory began in the mid-nineteenth century when Christian J. Thomsen, a Danish Scholar, for the first time in 1836 defined the past of human society in terms of technological and chronological stages marked by the successive use of tools made of stone, bronze and iron (called Three-Age System). In 1851, Daniel Wilson coined the term Prehistory, and in 1865 John Lubbock used the terms Palaeolithic and Neolithic to emphasize the change and progress in tool-types. Documentation of evidence for the Stone Age in India began with the first discovery of a hand-axe at Pallavaram near Madras (now Chennai) by Robert B.

Foote, called Father of Indian Prehistory, in 1863. Since then, particularly during the last five decades, there has been a significant progress in Indian archaeological studies which have enriched greatly our knowledge of the remote past of the Indian subcontinent (see next chapter).

Prehistory of India, as elsewhere, is divided into three broad periods — Palaeolithic (*paleo*-old, *lithic*-stone i.e., Old Stone Age), Mesolithic (*meso*-middle, *lithic*-stone, i.e., Middle Stone Age) and, Neolithic (*neo*-new, *lithic*-stone, i.e., New Stone Age). Each of these periods is marked by distinct features as well as gradual improvement in tool-making skill and technology. Thus, while the Palaeolithic period witnessed a shift from heavy and asymmetrical to flake-based tools, the Mesolithic period was characterized by the use of "microliths" or small "geometric tools" in the form of triangles, crescents, etc. The Neolithic period, the last phase of Prehistory, was marked by the use of polished and ground tools having better and sharper cutting edge. This period also witnessed the emergence of first farming communities, i.e., the communities which domesticated plants and animals, used pottery and lived in hut-like structures in different ecozones of the country.

Since tools and tool-technologies have a direct impact on the production capacity and material life of the human beings, gradual improvement in tool-types from Palaeolithic to Neolithic period is viewed as a primary factor which led to change in early human's subsistence pattern from hunting and gathering to food-production. This concept of reciprocal relationship between technological growth and material progress was first expounded by Gordon Childe (1892-1957) and later popularised by Braidwood and others. Childe used the term "Neolithic Revolution" to emphasize the dynamic impact which the beginning of farming and settled life had on human kind during the Neolithic period. But the new archaeological data tends to reveal that the transition to farming was one of gradualness and what one notices is more of a "transformation" or "evolution" rather than a "revolution" (see Chapter 5).

Environmental Factors

The physical environment is viewed by many scholars as a major determining factor which influenced the process of change and progress during the Prehistoric times. The physical environment is characterised by topography, climate and the nature of soil which in turn determine the fauna (animal life) and flora (vegetation) — the two primary sources of subsistence for the early humans.

Palaeolithic period covered the Pleistocene (Greek term for "most recent") or the "Ice-age" dated from around 2 m.y.a (million years ago) to 10,000 BP (Before Present). It was an age when a large part of the world was covered by ice-sheets and the climate was extremely cold and arid. As this climate could sustain only limited flora and fauna in the form of bushes and hedges, giant animals with thick and hairy skin, the human ancestors had limited food resources and they lived the life of hunter-gatherers or scavengers. But with the onset of Holocene (a Greek term for "recent") period in around 10,000 BP, there was a change in climate which became warm and wet, very much like the present one. It resulted in the melting of snow and the formation of rivers and forests; even the animals became smaller and swifter. This climatic change made available not only new resources but also created opportunity for early humans for production of cereals and domestication of animals, ultimately enabling them to move from hunting-gathering to food-production and settled life.

The theory that the change in early human's life pattern was on account of change in environment is known as **"environmental determinism."** In its essence it means that humans are a component element of physical environment, and their life and activities are conditioned and governed by it. However, this theory is not fully accepted presently. It is argued that physical surroundings do play an important role in determining human activities but it does not mean that we humans are passive robots helplessly programmed to act according to the climatic conditions. The physical environment permits and at times even restricts the use of certain resources, but a human being is capable enough to overcome the hurdles in the path of progress through his skill and endeavour. It is argued that many other factors, such as cultural traditions, i.e. earlier experience, cultural contact i.e., social and economic interaction with other contemporary social groups, and demographic profile, i.e., the need to feed larger number of people, are also possible factors which could trigger a change. In short, many factors in combination, not the physical environment alone, may encourage technological innovations leading to progress in material and cultural life.

It may be worthwhile to note here that Indian Prehistory, on the whole, presents a picture of "cultural continuum" — a process in which each step marks a further growth or evolution over the earlier one. There is nothing static about Indian society and, as in other parts of the world, lithic technology in India too evolved gradually from heavier to smaller and sharper tools, creating necessary conditions for stage-wise cultural growth.

Human Evolution and Indian Prehistory

Prehistory is intimately connected with the evolution of man and his efforts to survive in adverse environment through technological modification of his tools and weapons. Though the earth was formed around 4,600 m.y.a (million years ago) and organic life appeared in the form of algae or seaweed as far back as some 2,000 m.y.a., the man emerged much later as a result of a long and gradual process of biological change in the last geological epoch called Quarternary period which is subdivided into two phases — (i) Pleistocene and (ii) Holocene.

All humans, zoologically speaking, belong to a family called hominid, having the genus or structural characteristics called *homo*. Initially, they along with apes and gibbons formed a part of a group called the primates, the earliest order of mammals. At some point of time, the hominids, for uncertain reasons, diverged from the apes and gradually developed into modern man through various, now extinct, sub-species such as *Homo habilis* (handy-man), *Homo erectus* (upright-man) and *Homo sapiens* (wise-man).

From biological point of view, the human evolution was marked by three distinct functional features — (i) perfect bipedal instead of guadrupedal locomotion; it is associated with the modification of pelvis and lower extremities; (ii) changes in the upper part of the body; it resulted in rotating movement of the shoulders; and (iii) increase in the cranial capacity or brain size — the brain size of modern man is estimated to be 1200-1450 cc, roughly three times that of his most ancient ancestor. The significance of these changes is that whereas bipedalism permitted man to use hands, now freed from walking, to make and use tools, the brain size made him plan and evolve new strategies in search for food.

It is now generally believed that the oldest member of the human family who walked, though partially, on two legs appeared first in the tropical or sub-tropical belt of Africa, away from the ice-barrier, about 4 m.y.a. or may be even earlier. This bow-legged ape-man is called *Australopithecine africanus* (lit. Southern ape of Africa). His fossils have been recovered from various places in central and eastern part of Africa. Its upright position is indicated by the foot-prints found on cold lava-ash at Laetoli (Tanzania), and from the small skeleton of a female nick-named Lucy, discovered at Hadar (Ethiopia) in 1974. While the foot-prints are dated around 3.8 m.y.a., the "Lucy" skeleton is estimated to be 3.2 m.y. old. This species is not associated with any type of tools. The earliest known evidence of stone tools found in association with hominid fossils are reported from Hadar (Ethiopia) and are considered to be 2.3 million years old. These tools are made on pebbles by striking one against the other to get a sharp edge and are called Oldowan because such tools were first recovered from Olduvai Gorge, Tanzania. In spite of some difference of opinion, the scholars by and large agree with Leakey and Tobias, the anthropodogists, that these tools were the product of a later species called *Homo habilis* (the handy-man) who happen to be the earliest tool-makers. What is significant here is the recognition of the fact that around 2.5 m.y.a. human ancestors had started making tools which in the course of time gave them mastery over their environment. The *Homo habilis* survived from 2.5 m.y.a. to 1.5 m.y.a. when there developed a new species called *Homo erectus* from whom emerged ultimately *Homo sapien sapiens* around 40,000 BP (Before Present). An important feature of the human evolution is that with each new species we notice a progressive improvement and refinement in tool-types.

An important discovery made by early man was that of fire, traditionally ascribed to the *Homo erectus*. It provided him light, heat and protection from predators. It also enabled him to move out from the tropical areas to new places in a colder region. There is, however, considerable debate regarding the time and place where fire came to be used first. Some scholars find its earliest evidence in the lump of a burnt clay from Chesowanga (Kenya) dated 1.4 m.y.a., while others look for it in the caves of Swartkrans (South Africa) dated 1 m.y.a. But as there is no evidence of fire place at these places, it is difficult to assert that this fire was deliberate. It is suggested that better evidence of fire comes from the caves at Choukou-tien (China) where a piece of charcoal has been found in the context of 5,00,000 BC.

It is suggested that *Homo erectus* at one point of time moved out of their original homeland in Africa and colonised different places in Europe, Western Asia, China, South Africa, etc. where they developed subsequently into various local species such as Java man (Pithecanthropas), Peking man (Sinathropas), Neanderthal man of Europe, etc. This assumption is based on the study of early stone tools which show remarkable similarity across the globe. But not all scholars accept this view because the nature and factors of dispersal and diffusion from Africa are not clear. Besides, it is argued that human mind is so constituted and endowed that it may develop similar culture (tools and weapons) in similar ecological conditions without any necessary outside influence. The debate on this issue, however, is not fully settled yet.

As far as the Indian sub-continent is concerned, there is no definite evidence of the occurrence of a true hominid fossil. The fossils designated as *Ramapithecus* found in the Siwalik hills in north-western India in 1932 were at one time thought to be of a human ancestor but are now considered to have belonged to an ancestor of an orangutan. However, a large number of Palaeolithic tools and artifacts discovered over a large part of India do confirm the presence and activities of the early humans here. Some of the tools found at Riwat, near

Rawalpindi, are believed to be as old as 2 million years (see chapter-III).

The discovery of a skull-cap from Hathnora, 40 km from Hoshangabad in the Narmada Valley of Madhya Pradesh in 1982 marks an important land-mark in the study of Prehistoric cultures in India. This skull has been identified by some with that of a *Homo erectus*, while others believe that it is of an archaic *Homo sapiens*. Though the exact date of the skull of this so called "Narmada man" is not confirmed, its antiquity cannot be doubted as it is found in association with the Lower Palaeolithic tool-types such as hand-axes and cleavers (Chakrabarti: 1999: 49-51).

It may, however, be pointed out that at one time the peninsular India was joined together with South America, Africa and Australia in a supercontinent or a landmass called Gondwana land which supposedly began to drift apart during the geological time-period called the Mesozoic era (225 m.y.a. — 65 m.y.a.). The geological evidence for this land connection between currently separated continents comes from a study of glacial deposits indicating similarities in flora and fauna not found in northern hemisphere. It is thus not improbable that early humans and their tool-technologies might have evolved in Indian tropical or sub-tropical regions independently of the African species. But this view needs further investigation.

Scientific Dating and Related Techniques

An essential prerequisite to the study of Prehistory is the knowledge of a sound chronological framework. It is necessary for understanding and analysing the process of change and continuity in the evolution of human culture. For a long time, Prehistorians had to be satisfied with the traditional method of "relative chronology," the chronology based on the twin principles of stratigraphy and typology of tools, implements and other material remains. The principle of sratigraphy underlines that the lowest layer would be earlier in date than the one above it whereas typology suggests that material remains with more refined features should be treated later in date than those with less refined ones. It was also based on the concept that tools or pottery having similar form and fabric found at different sites should be treated as contemporary. But with the introduction of new scientific dating techniques since 1950, the archaeologists are now able to establish "absolute" or "chronometric chronology," based on specific time-frame. The new techniques may not still give us an exact date but in view of a long period of Prehistory even an approximation to within a few centuries may be considered satisfactory. Some of the most commonly used dating methods are as follows.

(i) Radiocarbon (C_{14}) Dating

It is the most widely used dating technique. It was introduced by an American physicist, W.F. Libby, in 1949 and is based on the principle that all living things such as humans, plants and animals contain a fixed proportion of C_{12} and C_{14}. After their death or decay, while C_{12} remains stable, C_{14} decreases at a steady rate, and if the ratio between C_{12} and C_{14} present in a sample is calculated, its original date can be specified. It was originally suggested that half-life of C_{14} was 5568 years, but later when cross-examined against **dendrochronology** (i.e. dating based on the growth of yearly rings on certain long-lasting trees, as old as 8,000 years, growing in America and elsewhere), it was found that it needed some correction or **calibration** and consequently its half-line now is estimated to 5730 years. (Half-line means half of the carbon will disappear in 5730 years, and half of the other half, i.e. one quarter will take another 5730 years, and so on). This correction has pushed back the original C_{14} dates by a few centuries on the basis of a duly prepared graph. Thus, for example, 3000 BC obtained earlier by C_{14} becomes 3700 BC upon calibration.

The main shortcoming of C_{14} dating or radiocarbon dating is that it could be used more effectively for a period going back to about 40 to 50 thousand years. Theoretically, the method could be applied for dates as old as 80,000 years but it becomes less accurate as the quantity of C_{14} surviving in samples tends to get very small. This problem has now been overcome by the introduction of a new technique called **AMS** (accelerated mass spectrometry). It requires as little as a milligram of carbon in a sample to provide a date. Another advantage of AMS is that the range of C_{14} dates can be safely extended as far back as 1,00,000 years ago.

(ii) Thermoluminescence Dating (abbreviated as TL dating)

While C_{14} dating technique could be used only on organic materials (bone, wood, etc.), the TL method is helpful in dating inorganic objects such as pottery, the most abundant material found at the archaeological sites. It is based on the principle that at the time of pottery making, the clay of which pottery is made entraps certain minerals having electrons, and if a piece of a particular sample is heated in the laboratory, it will release accumulated energy in the form of light which can be measured to indicate the period when it was first fired or baked.

(iii) Potassium-argon or K-AR dating

This method is used to determine the age of a rock by

measuring the proportion of potassium (K_{40}) and argon in the volcanic ash containing Prehistoric remains. With this method dates can be obtained for objects as far back as 5,000 m.y.a. (million years ago). It has made possible to date early human fossils and foot-prints in eastern Africa.

(iv) Palaeomagnetic dating

It is based on the analysis of particles contained in the sediments which can indicate the time when old rocks containing human artifacts or fossils were formed.

There are various other dating methods most of which are still in experimental or limited use. One of these is **Uranium Thorium (U-TH)** dating. It is based on measuring the radioactive decay of isotope of uranium, and has proved useful for dating an object belonging to a period from 5,00,000 — 50,000 years, which otherwise lies outside the time range of C_{14} dating. The **Electron Spin Resonance (ESR)** method is used for a material which decomposes when heated, and is thus useful for dating such objects as tooth enamel.

Besides wide-ranging scientific dating techniques, an archaeologist today is also utilizing many other scientific methods in discovering the past. The **Optical Emission Spectrometry**, for example, is a technique that is being used to analyse the trace element in artifacts, particularly beads, pottery and metals. It involves the excitation of atoms in a sample by means of a laser beam and measuring the wave length of light. It helps in identifying the source of raw material, and thus examining the trade contacts between different regions using the particular raw material or the finished product.

The **"micro-wear"** or **'use-wear analysis,'** developed in 1964 by a Soviet archaeologist, Semenov, involves examination of, under microscope, the traces of wear left on a stone implement. It makes it possible for an archaeologist to determine the purpose for which the particular tool was used, i.e., whether it was used for cutting a piece of wood or bone or meat.

The archaeological studies in recent years have also benefited from new techniques to locate the past material remains. A technique which has proved quite fruitful to the archaeologists is **Remote Sensing** from high altitude through LANDSAT (a name for a U.S. satellite that records earth's natural resources using a remote sensing apparatus). In this system scanners record infra-red radiation from earth's surface and convert them electronically into photographic images. Landsat imagery or photographs have been used to trace underground channels in different parts of the world, such as Mesopotamia and Egypt. In India, it has brought to light in Rajasthan an underground river bed identified with the course of the lost Sarasvati. Some time back, certain scientists from NASA (U.S.A.) released the photographs of an undersea landmass or geological formation connecting India with Sri Lanka, and identified it, though without any solid evidence, with the Ramasetu mentioned in the Ramayana.

A technique used for **underwater archaeology** is known as SONAR, a term that comes from the words "sound navigation and ranging." Normally, this device is used by warships and military aircraft to locate enemy submarines. It sends out sharp pulses of sound which are reflected back when they strike an object undersea, and these vibrations are recorded to calculate the range and direction of the object. It is greatly useful in promoting **marine archaeology** and has helped in locating shipwrecks and undersea sites in different parts of the world. In India, it was recently used to locate a "township" off the Bay of Cambay in Gujarat, and its data is being processed.

The development of new techniques in the field of microbiology, since 1980s, has led to greater interest in the study of DNA cells known as mitrochondria (mt DNA) which are only inherited from mothers. It is based on the examination of very small quantities of DNA extracted from bones and teeth, as opposed to soft-tissues, and has opened up the possibility of finding out the genetic differences or similarities between the fossil remains of early humans. M. Walpoff, for example, on the basis of his study has offered the view that modern humans may have emerged roughly simultaneously in different regions of the world [*The Origins of Modern Humans*, ed. Smith and Spencer, New York, 1984, 411-483]

In short, the use of various scientific techniques today has made it possible for the archaeologists to reassess their archaeological data in the light of better chronological framework. In this context it may be pointed out that new dates have given a blow to the old theory of "diffusion" propounded by such scholars as Gordon Childe who believed that the earliest evidence of agriculture and metal technology came from Mesopotamia, and it was from here that these spread later to other parts of the world. The new dates, however, suggest that there might have been different pockets or ecozones where these activities developed independently and simultaneously, not necessarily diffused from West Asia.

New Theoretical Perspectives

In the study of Prehistory, archaeology is the primary source of information. The terms Prehistory and Archaeology are in fact interlinked — while Prehistory is a period in the history of humanity for which there are no written records, archaeology is a method to excavate and recover the unwritten records of the past in the form of material remains of the early humans. However, excavation is just one aspect of archaeology. The excavated material is of no use if it is not interpreted and analysed to understand early man's mind and behaviour. In fact, as it is remarked, archaeology is not just digging up "things," it is digging up "people." Therefore an archaeologist has to interact with scholars from other disciplines such as anthropology, sociology, chemistry, zoology, etc. and follow a multi-disciplinary approach for a better and holistic understanding of the past.

Earlier the archaeologists followed what is called a cultural-historical or collection and narration approach. This approach puts emphasis on two features — (a) detailed description of the typology of tools and pottery, i.e., their shapes, forms and fabrics, and (b) the concept of diffusion which argues that such activities as tool-technology or pottery-making or agricultural production spread from one single core area to other regions. The excavated material was dated on the basis of their successive layers of deposits (called seriation) suggesting that the bottom-most layer was the earliest whereas the uppermost was the latest. It also argued that the inferior tool-types must be earlier in time than the more refined ones. The proponents of this approach also followed the concept propounded by Gordon Childe that the archaeological remains such as pots, implements, ornaments, etc., "constantly occurring together" reflect the "culture" of the people. In Indian context, Stuart Piggott and Wheeler were the main followers of this perspective, though even today it has not lost its favour with some.

Since 1950, on account of the use of scientific dating techniques and the discovery of many new sites, there has been a great progress in the field of prehistoric research. It has led to the broadening of the definition of archaeological culture. In 1960s the scholars such as Lewis Binford, Flannery and David Clark propounded a new methodological approach which once-called "new archaeology" is now termed as "**processual archaeology**." This approach focuses not on the mere physical description of tools, pottery and other material remains, but aims to analyse them to understand the process of socio-economic change and progress. It raises questions about the possible life-pattern of the ancient humans and then tries to look for their answers in the material remains. It attempts to deal with such diverse issues as mechanism of trade and exchange, social inequality, role of political authority, etc. It views culture as a "system" having various "sub-systems" or components such as society, economy, environments, and argues that it is the interaction and interrelationship between them that triggers the process of change.

An important feature of "processual archaeology" is that it proposes to utilize the knowledge from other disciplines, particularly anthropology (a branch of study which deals with the origin of man, his beliefs and customs), to analyze the Prehistoric material remains. It also draws parallel from **ethno-archaeology**, the study of existing societies using similar tools and artifacts as those of Prehistoric times. It may be noted that ethno-archaeology does not emphasize historical continuity of traditions but attempts to understand the limitations and opportunities offered by environment in which the early humans lived. The "processual archaeology" also puts great emphasis on the study of environment to determine the animal and vegetal food resources of the early man. Thus, subjects such as palaeobotany and palaeozoology are also drawn into the study of archaeology.

In recent years, there has come up a new school of thought called "post-processual," a term coined by a British archaeologist Ian Hodder in 1986. It does not favour the "processual method" which first raises hypothetical questions and then looks for their answers in the ancient remains. It advocates that the archaeology of a region should be viewed in the context of history of the people concerned rather than from an alien point of view. It believes that each area follows its own trajectory of development; and argues that the hardware, i.e., our brain may be the same but the "soft-ware," i.e., the cultural traditions are generated independently. The concept of "cognitive archaeology," i.e., the study of ancient remains and symbols to gain an insight into the mind, belief and ideology of the early humans is also emphasized. Another concept which is gaining ground today is "gender archaeology." It aims to present early woman as an active rather than passive partner in the process of cultural transformation, and tends to highlight her role in various activities such as agriculture, craft-production, religion, etc.

In short, with new approaches to the study of archaeology, the focus of investigation has shifted from mere narration and description of archaeological data to their interpretation from the perspectives of social, economic, political and religious behaviour of the early humans. In India, it was S.C. Malik who in 1968 first gave a call for a change in descriptive method and advocated an anthropological and analytical approach, but his plea went unnoticed. It was only after H.D. Sankalia examined the relevance of "new" archaeology in the Indian context in 1977 that more and more scholars began to follow it, and today it is reflected in the writings of such archaeologists as D.K. Chakrabarti, K. Paddayya, D.P. Agrawal, Ravi Korisettar, etc.

2

Indian Archaeological Studies During the Last Five Decades and their Significance

ARCHAEOLOGICAL research in India began officially from 1861 when a separate department of Archaeological Survey of India was established with A. Cunningham as its head. Although some random discoveries of lithic tools and Prehistoric structures were reported from various places before 1861, these were based on insufficient fieldwork and there was little idea of relating them to the overall progress of Prehistoric man in South Asia. Cunningham's appointment too was made not to carry out excavations but to locate and identify important places mentioned in the ancient texts, particularly in those of the Chinese pilgrims, Fahien and Hiuen-Tsang. A few Harappan seals did come to his knowledge but he could not comprehend their significance. It was with the appointment of Sir John Marshall as the Head of the Archaeological Survey of India in 1902 that there began a system of excavations. But again these excavations were concentrated primarily on early historic cities or the Buddhist sites. However, it was during his tenure that the spectacular discovery of Harappan Civilization was made during 1920-22. It may be mentioned that Mohenjodaro, the mega city of the Harappans was discovered during the course of an excavation of a Buddhist stupa.

Later, the appointment of Wheeler in 1944 brought about a major change in the archaeological studies in India. He introduced the proper technique of site exploration and excavation and put emphasis on the concept of cultural sequence and stratigraphy. He also undertook to train a number of Indian students in the field of archaeology, and it were these students, first and but foremost among them being H.D. Sankalia, who played an important role in promoting the cause of archaeology in India after independence.

Among the persons who are credited with initiating Palaeolithic studies in India, it is Robert Bruce Foote, a geologist, who occupies the most important position. He discovered a hand-axe belonging to the early Palaeolithic period at Pallavaram, near modern Chennai in 1863, and later reported similar tools from many other sites. His collections, published posthumously in 1916, gave the study of Indian Prehistory a "clearly visible window." A significant stride in Palaeolithic studies in India was made in 1930s when A. Cammiade and M.C. Burkitt highlighted the interrelationship between the stratigraphic profile of Prehistoric tools and the palaeoenvironment with regard to the artifacts collected from Andhra Pradesh. Later, de Terra and Patterson of the Yale-Cambridge university team to India (1939) went beyond the palaeoclimatic correlations and introduced a geochronological scale. They attempted to determine the chronological sequence of different tool-bearing terraces along the river Soan, a tributary of the river Indus in Pakistan, on the basis of glacial sequence or cycle of the "Ice-age." The above studies provided the base for further archaeological research in India after 1947.

During the past fifty years, there have been vibrant activity and vigorous developments in the field of archaeology. An increased number of explorations and excavations, better field work as well as multi-disciplinary approach have greatly enriched our knowledge on the Prehistory and Protohistory of the Indian subcontinent. The introduction of new scientific techniques of dating the past remains has also vastly enlarged our horizon. As a result the tool technology and its impact on the behaviour and activities of early humans have come to be studied more deeply. The process of transition from the stage of hunting and food-gathering to that of food-producing has also become quite clear. Prehistoric rock paintings as well as the south Indian Neolithic and Megalithic cultures too have acquired a new focus. But, the most important feature of the post-1947 archaeological studies has been to bring forth the significance of the Proto-historic period. This period which forms a bridge between the Prehistoric and the Early historical period was earlier treated as a "dark period" as there was no clear information available on it. Today the identification of different types of potteries such as Ochre Coloured Pottery (OCP) and Painted Grey Ware (PGW) has helped us to clear the mist and place it in a specific time-frame. The excavations since 1950 at various sites particularly in Western Uttar Pradesh have brought to light a complete profile of occupation from OCP to PGW to NBPW, from 1800 BC to 600 BC. The Protohistoric period thus represents a continuity in Indian history (see below).

Recent archaeological studies in India have begun to incorporate new methodologies and theoretical perspectives. Initially, archaeologists followed the "culture-history," i.e., the traditional collection and narration approach, but since 1970s they have been concentrating more and more on understanding the socio-economic aspects of Prehistoric man with the help of other disciplines such as anthropology, sociology, botany, etc. Two aspects which have been engaging their attention are the palaeoclimatic changes and the environmental setting, as these determine not only the food resources but also the availability of raw material needed for tools and implements. Gurdeep Singh [1974] on the basis of pollen analysis and salt lake profiles has attempted to highlight the climatic fluctuations between general aridity and wetness in Rajasthan in ancient past.

Earlier archaeology was dominated by the "diffusionists," the scholars who traced the origin and spread of most of the Indian Prehistoric cultural traits, such as lithic tools, pottery forms, agricultural activities, etc., to West Asia or sometimes to South-East Asia. Even the Harappan Civilization was seen as a secondary and derivative product of urban "Idea" from Mesopotamia. Today, the concept of diffusion either in terms of "idea" or "migration" from outside is being discarded, and attempts are being made to follow a "processual" approach to emphasize the indigenous nature of cultural growth. Even the question of introduction of iron technology in India from outside has become a matter of debate. Whereas most of the scholars ascribe it to the Indo-Aryans who came in groups from Central Asia to India, D.K. Chakrabarti [1992] argues that instead of viewing iron in India as a diffusion from outside, India may be treated as an independent and separate entity for the growth of iron technology.

The introduction of different scientific dating methods, particularly that of radiocarbon dating since 1950 and its calibrated graph, has greatly revolutionised the chronology of the archaeological data the world over, including India. These have led to the revision of many earlier dates. For example, an earlier published C_{14} date of 1950 BC when calibrated (on the basis of 5730 years as half-life of the carbon) is pushed back by 400 years to 2350 BC. It has an important impact on adjusting the dates of Harappan Civilization in particular as the new chronological table brings Harappan Civilization (2600 BC – 1900 BC) directly in line with the Mesopotamian Civilization which was once believed to be earlier in date and hence a source of inspiration for the growth of urban cities in the Indus region.

A significant event in the history of Indian archaeology in recent years has been the discovery of a fossil (a skull cap) of a *Homo sapiens* at Hathnora in the Narmada Valley. It is found in association with the Early Palaeolithic tools. Though it is a lone find, it does put India on the global map of hominid fossil finds. It may be mentioned that Prehistoric tools recovered from Riwat, south-east of Rawalpindi, have been dated by Rendell and others to as far back as 2 m.y.a. (million years ago). Though no fossil as old as that has been found so far, the presence of stone tools does confirm the existence of Prehistoric human species in this region in the remote past.

Another important development in the post-1950 archaeology in India has been a clear cut demarcation and identification of **Palaeolithic period** in three successive phases — Lower, Middle and Upper. The stratigraphic profiles of tools clearly indicate that these phases were marked by gradual, stage by stage, progress in type and technology of tools from chopper-chopping and hand-axe to flake-based tools. What is equally noticeable is a corresponding change in the preference of raw material, from quartzite in the Early Palaeolithic period to fine-grained stone in the Middle and Upper Palaeolithic periods. It was H.D. Sankalia who for the first time identified the Middle Palaeolithic tools at Nevasa (Distt. Ahmadnagar, Maharashtra) in 1950's.

There has also been a major expansion in our knowledge on the geographical and distributional pattern of the Palaeolithic sites. They have been reported from almost all over the country including the regions of Assam, Bengal and Orissa. This wide distribution has made it clear that Indian Prehistorical features may not be viewed as an isolated phenomenon but should be studied in different regional and ecological contexts. It has also led to the use of ethno-archaeology for better understanding of the Prehistoric past.

The Palaeolithic sites are being studied today not from the viewpoint of tool assemblages alone, and there are efforts to highlight the subsistence implications of these settlements in relation to local soils and vegetation. This concept termed as settlement-subsistence pattern, borrowed by archaeologists from geography, proposes to study the Prehistoric settlements on the basis of the size of sites or site-size hierarchy, their inter-spacing and distribution in relation to the resources (food and raw material) required by the early humans. Archaeological excavations reveal that there are certain regions which contain settlements of different sizes (small, middle and extensive) situated close to each other. It is taken to indicate that large settlements were centres of power, political or religious, while the smaller ones supplied the required resources, and in this way the whole area was integrated into one "unit." The functional areas for different activities such as cattle penning, butchering and tool-making within a site are also being identified. K. Paddayya's studies on Hunsgi in Karnataka [1982], M.K. Dhavalikar's on Inamgaon [1988] and U.C. Chattopadhyaya's on Middle Gangetic valley [1996] are some important contributions in this field. A related aspect which is being highlighted is that of site-catchment analysis as advocated by Vita-Finzi and Higgs [1970]. It is argued that early human settlements were based on the consideration of availability of resources lying within a radius of about ten km — a distance which early man could cover by walking to collect the resources and reach back home by the evening.

Microliths were discovered as early as the 19th century but it was only in 1950s and 1960s that H.D. Sankalia, after the excavations at Langhnaj and other places in Gujarat, brought to light their real significance. He ascribed them to a separate phase called, the **Mesolithic period**, a period of transition linking Upper Palaeolithic (also sometimes called Epipalaeolithic) with the Neolithic period. Today, a large number of Mesolithic sites, including Mohrana Pahara in Mirzapur (UP), have been reported from different parts of the country and they have added greatly to our information on the life pattern of the Mesolithic people. The burials, the earliest evidence of which in India comes from this period, along with the goods placed with the dead, help us in gaining an insight into the socio-economic behaviour and the ritual system of these people. An increase in the number and density of Mesolithic sites, viewed from the point of demographical changes, indicates increase in population during the Mesolithic period.

There has also been a better understanding on the nature and character of the **Neolithic cultures**. The identification of a large number of Neolithic sites all over the country, right from Mehrgarh (Baluchistan) in the west to Daojali Hading (Assam) in the east, and from Burzahom and Gufkral (Kashmir) in the north to Paiyampalli (Tamil Nadu) in the south has brought to light a pan-Indian character of the Neolithic cultures. Besides, the study of tool-types and pottery fabrics, the issues relating to the origin and spread of plant cultivation and animal domestication during the Neolithic times have also come into sharper focus.

Contrary to earlier views, the history of agriculture in the Indian subcontinent now begins at Mehrgarh around the seventh millennium BC. The excavations conducted here by

Jarrige in late 1970s have confirmed the indigenous growth of wheat-barley cultivation and cattle-sheep domestication. The Mehrgarh excavations which are treated as a land-mark in the history of Indian archaeology, have given a blow to the concept of "Neolithic Revolution" as propounded by G. Childe because it is now clear that the transition from food-gathering to food-cultivation was gradual and not sudden.

The evidence of agricultural activities has also come from other regions in northern and southern India, though it is later in date. G.R. Sharma and his team in 1970s brought to light the evidence of rice at Koldihwa (Distt. Allahabad, UP) where rice-husk was found embedded in the clay of a number of potsherds. It has led many scholars to argue that rice might have been an indigenous crop rather than an import from China or South-East Asia. The cultivation of wheat, barley and rice at Chirand (Distt. Saran, Bihar) has been confirmed by the recovery of the grains of these crops in charred condition.

The discovery of Stone Age sites in the Mid-Gangetic Valley marks an important chapter in the Indian archaeological studies during the post-1950 period, as earlier nobody could believe that such sites could exist in a region where stone is not available locally. These sites, according to G.R. Sharma [1980], indicate early human's ability to adjust to a particular environment by bringing the raw material of stone from some distance or by using more of bone tools.

A large number of sites excavated in south India have now made it possible to formulate a coherent pattern of chronological and regional variations within the Southern Neolithic. The nature and character of the "ashmounds" is also being debated in a broader context of South Indian Prehistory. Since 1960s, there are attempts to highlight the interrelationship between the South Indian Neolithic Cultures and the village cultures further north, i.e. the Deccan Chalcolithic Cultures which used primarily Neolithic tools, and very little copper.

The studies on the **Megalithic cultures** in India have also come a long way since the excavation by Wheeler at Brahmagiri in 1947-48. A large number of Megalithic sites have been discovered all over the country, maximum number of which are in the peninsular India. Today there is enough data base to understand the chronology and the character of the Megalithic people who used iron tools and Black-and-Red ware. Earlier studies based on the mere description of types and forms of Megaliths have been superceded by studies highlighting the socio-economic and religious implications of the mortuary practices of the builders of Megaliths. The interrelationship between the Megalithic Culture and the succeeding cultures as represented in the Sangam literature is also being highlighted.

It may be noted that progress in studies on **archaeobotany**, the study of food-grains recovered in archaeological excavations, and archaeozoology, the study of animal remains found in archaeological excavations have been of great help in enhancing our knowledge on the Prehistoric agricultural and animal husbandry. While presence of stone querns and grinding stones indicate indirectly the use of food-grains by a particular group of people, the technique of flotation (the process of recovering carbonised seeds or grains by adding water to the soil and sieving it), which is being used increasingly since 1970 has been quite beneficial in having an exact idea of the type of food-grains which were cultivated and used. Vishnu-mittre, M.D. Kajale and others have made a valuable contribution in this field. Dorian Fuller on the basis of a large number of floating samples collected from different sites in south India has tried to explain the crop pattern among the south Indian Neolithic cultures. The archaeobotanical studies have generated a fresh debate among the Prehistorians as to which crops are indigenous to India and which are foreign in nature [Karisettar etc: 2002: 151 ff].

Similarly, the studies on **archaeozoology** are gaining ground to understand the man-animal relationship in the context of a particular region and environment. P.K. Thomas, for example, on the basis of his studies on the faunal data collected from various Prehistoric sites has highlighted the fact that animal domestication in the Indian subcontinent may go back to the Mesolithic times, much ahead of agricultural activity. It may be noted that the recovery of an ostrich egg-shell from Patne (Maharashtra) indicates that this giant bird which once roamed around in India during the Upper Palaeolithic period became extinct later, probably because of climatic changes.

The progress made in **archaeobiology** has also added a new dimension to our perspective. Earlier human skeletons were studied primarily to identify their physical features with regard to different races, viz., Negroloid, Mongoloid, etc. This approach is, however, losing favour and now efforts are being directed towards understanding the human remains in the context of wider issues relating to biological affinities, the impact of changing food habits on human osteology (bone structure), migration and intermixing of the people, etc. K.A.R. Kennedy and J.R. Luckacs are prominent among those scholars who are focussing on these aspects of archaeobiology in India.

The research on Prehistoric **rock art** during the last three decades has grown from stray individual studies to an organised effort by a number of scholars. The painstaking survey and documentation of a large number of rock art sites in central India by V.S. Wakankar in 1970s is considered as an important turning point in this context. Rock art represents not only the aesthetic activity but also furnishes an evidence of the subsistence pattern and socio-religious activities of the early humans. Indian Prehistoric rock art has received today an international recognition and the site of Bhimbetka which contains the maximum number of rock shelters and paintings in India has acquired a status of a World Heritage Site.

In recent decades, beads made of organic material (bone, ivory, shell) or of stones (agate, carnelian, etc.) are also being treated as an evidence of Prehistoric art. The bone beads recovered from Kurnool caves in south India and the ostrich egg-shell beads from Patne in Maharashtra have been dated back to 25000 BC to 12000 BC (Upper Palaeolithic period). These are regarded as the earliest evidence of "portable" art in India. The beads are considered not just as symbols or expressions of love and beauty but are also studied to draw information on the sources of their raw material, centres of production, manufacturing technology, exchange mechanism, etc. Kenoyer and Vidale have made important contribution to the studies on bead technology during the Harappan times.

The Indus Civilization or the **Harappan Civilization** as it is called now, has been engaging the attention of scholars all over the world ever since it was discovered in 1920-22. Large scale excavations and fresh data since 1950 have not only added to our information but have also cleared the mist on many questions regarding the origin and decline of this civilization. Today, the Harappan civilization is no more considered as an import from outside whether in the form of migration of people or an "idea" nor its decline attributed to "massacre" committed by the in-coming Indo-Aryans. The whole process of its rise and fall is now viewed against the backdrop of internal dynamics of change demarcated in three phases, viz., Early Harappan (3500 BC –2600 BC; rural), Mature Harappan (2600 BC – 1900 BC; urban) and Late Harappan (1900 BC – 1400 BC; rural). It is also now evident that the Harappan Civilization did not "collapse" or disappear all of a sudden but was gradually transformed into a rural culture with no big structures, specialized craft or exchange system. A large number of Late Harappan sites discovered in Punjab, Haryana and western Uttar Pradesh demonstrate more than anything else that the Harappan people after the decline of their cities were on a major move towards the east. Almost the same picture is suggested by the map of the Late Harappan Gujarat where a move was towards Malwa region. The overlapping of Late Harappan pottery with the Painted Grey Ware (PGW), ascribed to the Indo-Aryans, at certain sites such as Dadheri (Ludhiana) and Katpalon and Nagar (Distt. Jullundhar) in Punjab is taken as an indication of coexistence of Late Harappans with the local people.

The identification of a large number of new Harappan sites in India and Pakistan since 1950 has led to a better picture of the extent of Harappan Civilization, and it is now regarded as the largest among the Bronze Age Civilizations in the ancient world. Rafiq Mughal's researches in the region along the river Hakara (Ghaggar-Saraswati course, called so in Pakistan territory) in Cholistan have revealed that there was a major concentration of Harappan sites in this area too. Harappan sites are being studied on the basis of their functional utility and have been designated as port towns, trading outposts, factory sites, etc.

The earlier view based on the Mesopotamian model that the Harappan Civilization was an "empire" under the rule of a "Priest-king" is also being discarded. Instead, it is now viewed by many scholars as a combination of a number of "domains" or regional centres closely related to their hinterland to procure necessary resources.

There has also been a better understanding on the nature and character of the Harappan urbanisation. For example, the discovery of a ploughed field at Kalibangan (Rajasthan) and of a terracotta model of a ploughshare from Banawali (Haryana) confirm that the Harappan cities had a strong agricultural base. A subject which has come under sharper focus these days is the internal and external trade contacts of the Harappan people. The discovery of a Persian Gulf seal at Lothal by S.R. Rao in 1950s and the archaeological excavations in the Persian Gulf region by Tosi and others in the last two decades have tended to highlight the role of Oman (Makan of the Mesopotamian inscriptions) as an important intermediary in the Indo-Mesopotamian trade.

The archaeological findings during the last fifty years have thus greatly enlarged our vision on various aspects of the Harappan civilization. However, two important issues which are being hotly debated among the historians and the archaeologists presently are, a) the nature of Harappan legacy, i.e. whether the Harappan socio-religious traditions continued to survive in one form or the other in later periods or not, and b) the authorship of the Harappan Civilization, i.e., whether the credit of founding the glory of the Harappan Civilization should be attributed to the Sanskrit-speaking Indo-Aryans or to the Dravidian-speaking local people. The crucial point on which the authorship debate hinges is the question of the presence or the absence of horse (an animal dear to the Indo-Aryans) during the Harappan times. While most of the historians argue that true horse came to India with the Indo-Aryans who immigrated from Central Asia in around 1800 BC, many archaeologists insist on having identified the horse remains from various Harappan sites including Surkotda.

Though Harappan Civilization continues to be an important subject of interest, there has been after 1950 a shift in focus from north-west to the Gangetic plains on the one hand and the Deccan and south India on the other. And one of the most important results of it, as mentioned earlier, has been to bring into light the Chalcolithic period of Indian history — the period of which there had been no clear evidence earlier. It could become possible because of the systematic integration of archaeological data from various sites in Central India, Deccan and western Uttar Pradesh, i.e., the region outside the Harappan influence. The importance of Chalcolithic period lies in the fact that it represents the continuum of human endeavour in Indian subcontinent right from the end of the Harappan cities in around 1900 BC to the rise of cities or "Second Urbanisation" in the Gangetic valley in the sixth century BC.

The **Chalcolithic Cultures** in Central India and the Deccan were first brought to light by Sankalia's excavations at Jorwe (Distt. Ahmadnagar, Maharashtra) in 1950s. As more and more sites of similar nature came to be discovered over a wider area later, the picture on the life-pattern of the Chalcolithic people tended to become better. M.K. Dhavalikar [1988] made a detailed study of the local subsistence base and the environmental setting of the Chalcolithic people of Inamgaon (Distt. Pune) — the chief site of the Jorwe culture in the Deccan.

The **Copper Hoards** (called so because a variety of copper tools comprising axes, harpoons, etc., have been found in hoards) were reported earlier but their cultural significance came to be recognised only in 1950s when a large number of these were discovered from Bisauli, Rajpur Parasu and other places in western Uttar Pradesh. As these hoards were found located below the PGW levels of iron using people, their correlation with the copper using OCP people (see below) is almost accepted. However, their authorship is still a matter of debate.

Studies on **potteries** since 1950s have also acquired a new dimension. For a long time pottery was classified on the basis of its form and texture, and its origin, spread and chronological sequence was explained on the basis of its similarity with those found in other regions. But now it is being treated more as a means to highlight the change and continuity in material life of the people in the light of contemporary literature. Thus, for example, while OCP has been associated with the copper-using Rigvedic culture (1500 BC – 1000 BC), the PGW has been identified with the iron-using Later Vedic people. Similarly, NBPW, a pottery much better in form and fabric, has been regarded as an important component of the urban life in the sixth century BC. The excavations since 1950 at various sites in the Upper Gangetic region, such as Hastinapur, Atranjikhera (Distt. Etah), Kaushambi and also at Jodhpura (Distt. Jaipur) and Noh (Bharatpur) in Rajasthan, have revealed a complete profile of occupation from OCP to PGW to NBPW periods. Incidentally changing pottery traditions also indicate a shift in the centre of socio-economic activity from the Upper Gangetic (eastern Haryana and western Uttar Pradesh) to a more fertile Middle Gangetic region (eastern U.P. and Bihar).

Among the important pottery types, Ochre Coloured Pottery (**OCP**) was first reported by B.B. Lal from Badaun and Bijnore districts of western Uttar Pradesh, and later many more OCP-related sites came to be discovered. OCP is thick and ill-fired, and is called so because on rubbing it leaves reddish colour on fingers. It is suggested that this phenomenon is because of its having been lying in the water-logged area for a long time. The archaeological evidence reveals that OCP people used copper but had no knowledge of iron. If Copper-Hoards are to be attributed to the OCP people, as it has been done, it may be presumed that they were adept in the field of copper technology. Since western U.P. does not have copper mines, it can be fairly assumed that copper must have been acquired from Khetri mines of Rajasthan or the Kumaon hills of Uttranchal or elsewhere. Some Thermoluminescence (TL) dates give OCP a wide range from 2650 BC – 1180 BC, but it is mostly dated to the second millennium BC.

Similarly, Painted Grey Ware **(PGW)** though noticed first at Ahicchatra in Western U.P. in the mid-1940s, its cultural significance came to be realized only in 1950s when B.B. Lal excavated Hastinapur. On the basis of the evidence of flood at this site, B.B. Lal put forward the hypothesis that PGW culture represented the period of Mahabharata because, as per the reference in the text, people of Hastinapur deserted the town and migrated to Kaushambi because of the floods.

PGW is a smooth surfaced grey coloured pottery with paintings in form of dots, lines, etc. in black. Clay used for the ware is of high quality. It is made on a fast rotating wheel for thinness. Its flawless finish along with uniform texture and colour suggest a better firing technique and indicate a great improvement on the earlier OCP. It is distributed over a vast area extending up to Ujjain in south and Kaushambi in east but is largely concentrated in western U.P.. It is dated from 1100 BC to 600 BC, and thus coincides with the Later Vedic period of Indian history.

The presence of iron tools and weapons in the form of arrowheads, spearheads, daggers, and also chisels, sickles, axes, etc. at the PGW levels indicates that iron came to be used in a regular way for war, hunting and agricultural activities from the PGW period. Apart from Hastinapur and Kaushambi, Jakhera (Distt. Etah, U.P.) is an important PGW site. It has yielded various iron tools and implements such as sickles, hoes and ploughshare. The evidence of storage jars suggests surplus production necessitating storage of grains [Sahi: 1994]. The use of iron, as it is normally believed, led to the clearance of forests, growth of agricultural production and the movement of people towards the Middle Gangetic Valley which later became the focal point of political as well as social, economic and religious activities in the sixth century BC.

The significance of Northern Black Polished Ware **(NBPW)** and its relationship with the material progress in the form of trade, craft and towns in India from the sixth century BC onwards has also acquired a greater focus over the last fifty years. NBPW is a ware of a very fine quality with a thin black slip (coating with a semifluid clay). The most important characteristic feature of this ware is its mirror like polish which can't be easily scratched. It appears to be very expensive and highly prized as is evident from the copper riveting joining the broken parts of a vessel found at Ropar. It must have been used by the people of higher strata. It is dated from 600 BC – 200 BC. It is distributed over a vast area extending from Somnath in Gujarat to Chandraketugarh and Tamluk in West Bengal, but it is mainly concentrated in the Middle Gangetic Valley (Allahabad-Patna region). NBPW is found along with the earliest metallic coins, called Punch-marked coins, indicating economic progress during the period.

Reference may also be made to fresh light that is being shed on the origin and nature of the **Rouletted Ware**. It is a distinctive ceramic which was first noticed by Wheeler at

Arikamedu, an important Indo-Roman centre of trade during the early centuries of the Christian era, situated near Pondichery. It is made of extremely fine and well-levigated clay and has a thin fine slip. The most distinctive feature of it is its decoration in two or three lines of rouletted (dotted) pattern produced by rotating a toothed wheel. Wheeler argued that it was not an Indian feature and therefore designated it as a Roman pottery. This view is now being controverted as at several sites this pottery occurs in a period much earlier than the beginning of the Roman trade in the Ist century AD. At Chandraketugarh (24 Pargana Distt., W. Bengal), it goes back to the Mauryan period in the third century BC. Moreover, the trace element analysis of its mineral contents had led V.D. Gogte to argue that the Rouletted ware was probably made in Tamluk-Chandraketugarh region of West Bengal from where it was sent to other areas. It is, therefore, likely that this ware is an Indian invention from where it went to the Mediterranean region rather than vice-versa.

As with pottery, the subject of **metals and metallurgy** is also being studied more deeply to understand their socio-economic implications. In this field, N.R. Bannerji [1965], and D.K. Chakrabarti [1992] D.P. Agrawal [2000] have made valuable contributions. Copper and iron tools are being studied from various viewpoints such as their resource areas, the technology of smelting and forging (heating metal to make it soft to hammer into desired shape) etc. Though there is some controversy among scholars, as noted earlier, on the origin and spread of iron technology in India [Chakrabarti: 1992] it is normally accepted that the development in iron technology was an important factor in the growth of trade and towns in the mid-Gangetic valley in the sixth century BC.

As far as **historical archaeology** is concerned, it may be mentioned that there has not been as much progress in this field as it should have been, but even then the excavations at a number of towns have yielded quite useful information. For example, the excavations at Arikamedu, Alagankulam, Kaveripattinam, etc. have confirmed the significant role that Tamil Nadu coast was playing in the Indo-Roman trade during the early centuries of the Christian era. Rich structures and Roman gold coins found at Kushan and Satavahana levels in northern India and the Deccan offer an evidence of economic progress during the first and second centuries AD. At the same time, poor structures and paucity of coins as reported in the archaeological excavations in the mid-Gangetic Valley have made R.S. Sharma to postulate a disturbed economic condition leading to the growing tendency of feudalism during the Gupta and post-Gupta periods. The discovery of beads of semi-precious stones such as agate and carnelian in the recent excavations in Burma, Malaysia and other places has pushed back the antiquity of India's contact with South-East Asia as far back as 500 BC.

In short, intensive field work as well as new analytical approaches during the last fifty years have greatly enlarged our geographical and conceptual horizons on Indian Prehistory and Protohistory. Archaeological studies have come considerably away from the past tradition of collection and narration of archaeological data to focus on various other features such as ecology and environment, settlement and subsistence patterns and other subjects to reconstruct the early human behaviour in a holistic manner.

3

Palaeolithic Cultures

Introduction

THE Palaeolithic period or the Old Stone Age constitutes the longest phase of Prehistory and covers the whole range of the Pleistocene epoch from about 2 m.y.a. to 10,000 BP. In this period, the early humans, who shared the landscape with various wild and giant animals or megafauna such as buffalo, rhino, tiger, elephant, etc., started making stone tools to survive in a hostile environment.

The Palaeolithic Age is divided into three cultural phases, viz. Early or Lower Palaeolithic, Middle Palaeolithic, and Late or Upper Palaeolithic. This division is based on progressive improvement in tool-types which gradually came to acquire better efficiency in their cutting edge and operating ease. Thus, while Lower Palaeolithic period was marked by the use of heavy pebble tools, termed as chopper-chopping tools and hand-axes, the Middle Palaeolithic was characterised by tools made on flakes, and Upper Palaeolithic by sharp blades and burins. These tools, with some regional variations, exhibit remarkable similarity in their form, technique and raw material all over the Indian subcontinent.

It must be pointed out that transition from one stage to another was not sudden, and, wherever clear stratigraphic profiles are available, a clear evolution of lithic industry undergoing transformation from Lower to Middle to Upper Palaeolithic is noticeable. De Terra and Patterson of the Yale and Cambridge mission (1939) found in the valley of River Soan, which flows near Rawalpindi in Pakistan, five different terraces containing tools which were, in initial stages, heavier and cruder but progressively became thinner and finer. Similarly, in the Belan Valley (the region from Allahabad to Varanasi) a complete sequence of stone age cultures from the Lower Palaeolithic to the Neolithic, and even to the Chalcolithic is noticed. Bhimbetka, near Bhopal in Madhya Pradesh, too has yielded evidence of continuous Prehistoric occupation from the Early Palaeolithic and Middle Palaeolithic to the Mesolithic period. Patne, in Distt. Jalagaon in Maharashtra, also shows continuous sequence of Stone Age cultures from Middle Palaeolithic to the Mesolithic Age.

Our knowledge of the exact function of most of the Palaeolithic tools, in spite of the micro-wear analysis, is quite imperfect but it seems certain that they served a variety of purposes like hunting, butchering, skinning of animals, digging of roots and making wooden tools or weapons.

Chronology

The earliest stone tools in India are pebble tools and their evidence comes from Riwat, south-east of Rawalpindi in Pakistan. These tools on the basis of Palaeomagnetic dating have been dated by Rendell and Denell to around 2 m.y.a. It is a significant discovery as it puts Prehistoric tools found in India at par with those in Africa. A related evidence of tools comes from Dina and Jalalpur in the Jhelum basin (Pakistan) where the assemblage is believed to be 1.2 million to 2 million year old. Sometime back, the tools found at Bori, Distt. Pune in Maharashtra were considered to be 1.38 m.y. old but, after rigorous examination, the date of these tools is believed to be around 6,70,000 year ago. Though the debate on the date of these tools is still not over, the Bori tools are important as they represent the earliest artifacts in the interior of the subcontinent away from the north-western region. Thus, though the earliest tools in the Indian subcontinent are believed to be as old as 2 m.y.a., most of the early Palaeolithic tools, broadly speaking, belong to a period from around 6,00,000 to 1,50,000 BP, while those of Middle Palaeolithic and Upper Palaeolithic Ages are dated between 1,50,000 to 40,000 BP and 40,000 to 10,000 BP, respectively. The tool-types of the above three phases are believed to represent the technological skill of the three different human species, viz. *Homo erectus, Homo sapiens, Homo sapien sapiens.*

It may be noted that chronological framework as mentioned above provides just a working basis for studying the large assemblage of tools and weapons as it is difficult to fix a definite dividing line for the periods so remote in time. The dates may vary from site to site, but what is significant is that they indicate the presence of different phases of Palaeolithic Cultures in India in the Pleistocene period or the Ice-Age.

Tools and Technologies

The lithic tools form the primary source of our information regarding early human's activities and behaviour, his culture and tradition. Lithic technology, like any other craft, is a combination of two factors: the first is planning, i.e., to draw up a picture in mind and think of a method to make a tool out of a given raw material, and the second is technique, i.e., the use of hands and fingers to give the tool a desired shape. The Prehistoric man, who was primarily interested in fabricating stone tools having pointed end or sharp cutting edge, came to learn the art of making desired tools gradually through hit and trial mechanism. The texts on Prehistory refer to a number of lithic techniques, such as anvil or block-on-block technique, free hand-held technique, Clactonian technique, Levallosian technique, Mousterian technique, etc., — the last three being named after the European sites where similar type of tools were first found. However, broadly speaking, there are basically three tool making techniques which can be decribed

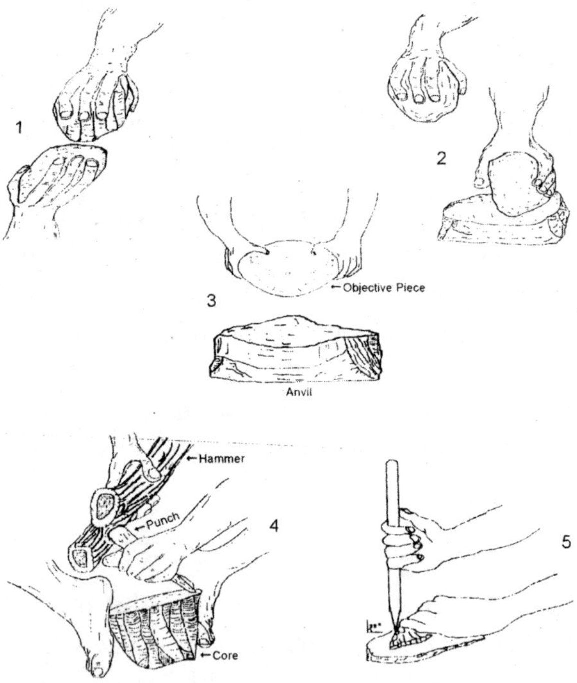

Prehistoric Tool Techniques —
1 to 3 forms of direct percussion technique; 4 indirect percussion technique; 5 pressure technique

Fig. 1

(Modified after Sinha : 1999)

as based on percussion or direct percussion, indirect percussion and pressure application. Each of these refers to a varying degree of force applied on the core to make a tool of a desired shape **(see Figure 1)**.

In direct percussion technique, a stone/pebble was hit perpendicularly on the edge of another stone to produce a big and massive flake with wide angles or zig-zag edges. Gradually, in the course of time, the early man learnt to control his strokes and, directing his blows at a specific angle near the edge of a stone, he was able to produce flakes with sharper and better cutting edge. What is important is that by now the early man was able to understand the difference between the core and flake tools. Flakes were those pieces which were removed from a large block either by hard hammer (stone) or soft hammer (the one made of bone, antler or hard wood), while core tools were those from which flakes were removed. Man also realized that flakes could be further retouched to acquire a shape or an edge for a specific job. Thus, while earlier tools were all-purpose implements, the later ones became job or task specific.

In indirect percussion technique, the pressure on the core is put not directly but indirectly through an object of either stone or bone or hard wood to take out the flakes of desired shape or size. The pressure technique, on the other hand, refers to the method in which flakes are removed not by hitting, directly or indirectly, but by putting pressure at one specified point to make flakes jump out of the core. The flakes thus produced could be retouched further to obtain a desired shape such as that of scrapers, borers or awls. This technique was more suitable for use on softer and fine-grained stones like agate, chert, etc., which came to be used as a raw material in the Middle and Upper phases of the Palaeolithic period. There are certain sites in Hunsgi Valley (Karnataka) and Belan Valley (U.P.) which have been characterised as "factory sites," i.e. the sites where tools were made of local raw material and sent to other places [R. Korisettar: 2002: 24, 30]. It may suggest the beginning of some sort of barter exchange among the Prehistoric societies.

Many of the lithic techniques followed by the Prehistoric man in India are named after the French or other European sites, for example, Acheulian after St. Acheul and Levallosian after Levallois, both in France where particular types of tools were discovered first. These terms, it may be noted, just indicate similarity in tool-types and do not imply any cultural connection or diffusion from these areas. But it is certainly amazing that Indian tool-types are so similar to those from Africa and Europe that one really wonders how such uniformity could be achieved in such distant time and space. Whether it should be attributed to the migration of idea or of the people from outside or to the indigenous and independent process, it can't be said definitely, but the possibility of indigenous growth of Indian tool-types is far more greater.

The Early Palaeolithic period was marked by two types of tool cultures and these are known as the Soan or Sohan culture, named after River Soan, a tributary of the Indus in Potwar Plateau of northern Pakistan, and the Acheulian culture, named after the site of St. Acheul (France). The Soan culture was represented by pebble-based tools called chopper-chopping tools and formed the chief lithic tradition in the sub-Himalayan region, i.e. north and north-western India. The Acheulian culture, on the other hand was characterised by the tools called hand-axes and cleavers. Once known as the "Madrasian" Culture, as hand-axes were first discovered near erstwhile Madras in 1863, it was a popular tool-making tradition in peninsular India. Earlier these two traditions were believed to be distinct but as some hand-axes have been found in northern region as well, it has been argued by Mohapatra [1990: 251-60] that these two were part of the same cultural tradition and whatever difference we notice in their form is on account of difference in ecological setting and the availability of raw material.

As far as chopper and chopping tools are concerned, the main distinction between the two types is that choppers are worked on one side and are thus "unifacial," while the chopping-tools are worked on both sides and are "bifacial," though both seemed to have served the same purpose of either chopping a tree or a piece of flesh from an animal body. These tools were acquired by direct percussion or straight hitting. In the next stage we notice another tool-type called hand-axe, an axe used by hand rather than with a handle. It occupies the most significant position in the Early Palaeolithic period. It is basically a core-tool and was produced by knocking off flake systematically from several directions by the use of either hard or soft hammer. It is a heart or pear shaped piece with a thick blunt butt or holding end, and a tapering working end to form a point. There are many types of hand-axes, identified according to their shapes and fabrication techniques, but the most important one is known as Acheulian. It is shorter, neater and has a strikingly symmetrical shape than other types known as Clactonian or Abbevillian (named after European sites). Another important tool which occurs regularly in the Early Palaeolithic context is called cleaver. It is a flat tool made from a big rectangular flake and has a broad axe like cutting edge. Sometimes it has a U-shape to the entire cutting edge of the tool **(see Figure 2)**.

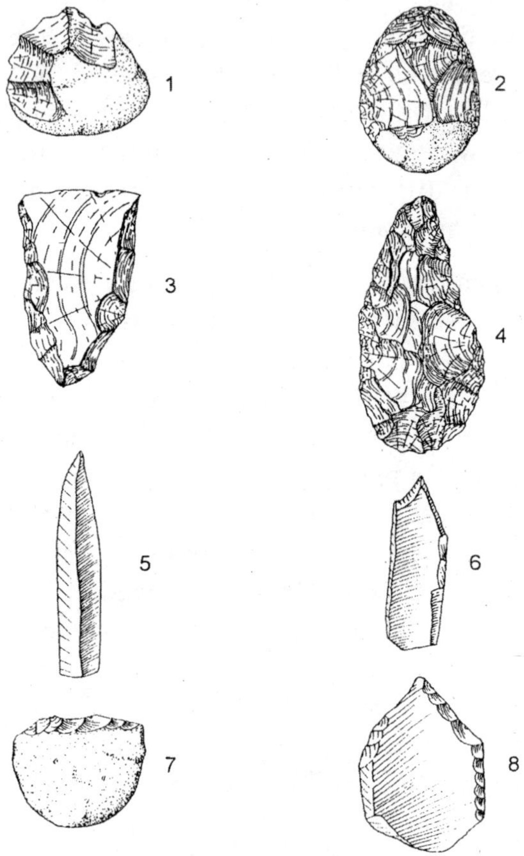

Palaeolithic Tools —
1. Chopping tool; 2. hand axe made from pebble; 3. cleaver made from large flake; 4. hand axe; 5. blade; 6. burin; 7 & 8 scrapers

Fig. 2

The choice of **raw material** used for tool-making varied from region to region and depended upon its availability. Thus, in the Early Palaeolithic period whereas quartzite, which is widely available in different hill ranges in India, was used over much of the country, in Maharashtra basalt and in Hunsgi region of Karnataka limestone were preferred. But interestingly, the tools, though made of different materials, present a picture of remarkable similarity in form and techniques.

The Middle Palaeolithic period was marked by further advance in tool-making technology. It was characterised by the use of tools made on medium-sized flakes. These tools were thinner and smaller than those of Early Palaeolithic period and were largely made on fine grained material like agate, jasper and chert. The chopper-chopping tools become extinct, and hand-axes and cleavers are rare.

The assemblages now comprise a variety of scrapers, borers and points. A scraper was a tool which was manipulated by the force of fingers rather than that of palm as in the case of hand-axe. The predominant technique followed in the Middle Palaeolithic period is known as Levallosian, named after a French site. In this technique, the core was first dressed or trimmed to obtain a flat surface or a "tortoise" shape, and flakes of desired size were produced after hitting at a specific point preferably by a soft-hammer made of bone or hard wood. In this way, symmetrical and thinner flakes were obtained. This process indicates greater insight and forethought on the part of early humans. These flake-based tools were first identified in 1956 by H.D. Sankalia at Nevasa in Maharashtra, and he provisionally named them as "Nevasa Culture," but subsequently excavations at other places revealed that these tools were not a local phenomenon but formed a general feature of the Middle Palaeolithic Cultures spread over different regions in India.

The Upper Palaeolithic period notices further reduction in size and weight of the tools. This phase is dominated by tool types described as flakes and burins. Burin is a chisel like tool made on a blade-like flake. It has a sharp and straight cutting edge of a common screw driver and could be used for making grooves in a wooden or bone handle to fix the blades. The elongated flakes with deliberately worked sharp edge have been called as knife or knife-blades. The technique used in the Upper Palaeolithic period was that of pressure flaking, a technique in which pressure was applied by chisel-like stone so that parallel sided blades with regular width and thickness would jump off the core material. This technique not only yielded smaller tools with better cutting edges but also led to less wastage of precious raw material. The blades or flakes thus made could be further retouched or trimmed to form an arrow or a harpoon. The main advantage of the Upper Palaeolithic tools, according to Allchin [1997: 74], was that being lighter they could be carried over a long distance, if necessary, far from their sources of supply or "factory sites." The use of bone tools formed an important feature of the Upper Palaeolithic age in Europe, but in India these tools in the shape of scrapers, chisels, etc., have been reported only from the cave called Muchchatta Chintamani Gavi at Kurnool in Andhra Pradesh. Therefore, as Chakrabarti points out [1999: 78], it is not known whether bone tools formed a component of Upper Palaeolithic man's tool-kit at other places in India too or their use was limited to this part of Andhra alone. A significant aspect of the Upper Palaeolithic technology was the choice and selection of raw material. The use of soft and fine grained stones had already begun but it became so important in this period that, with rare exceptions, this was the only material which was being utilized whether available in the nearby areas or not. This is evident from sites in the Belan Valley which reveal that the stone was brought from mid-Soon Valley at some distance [Prakash Sinha: 1999: 150]. It clearly indicates the beginning of some sort of exchange system in the Prehistoric times.

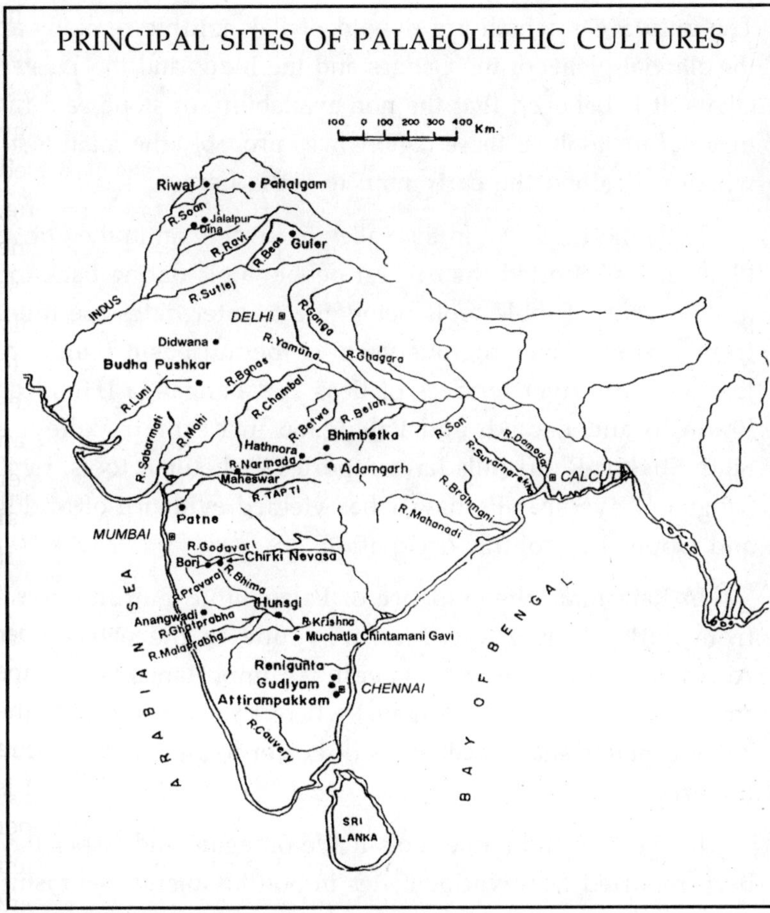

Fig. 3

Spread and Distribution of Palaeolithic Sites

The explorations and excavations over the last few decades have brought to light a large number of Palaeolithic sites **(see Figure 3)**. These are spread almost all over the Indian subcontinent, from the foot-hills of the Himalayas in the north to Tamil Nadu in the south, and from Peshawar and Sind in the west to Meghalaya (Garo Hills) and Bengal in the east.

The only areas which are devoid of Palaeolithic remains are the alluvial plains of the Ganges and the Indus and the Western Ghats. It is believed that the non-availability of stone as a raw material for tools in these regions was probably the main factor which restrained the early man to settle here.

In the north, Riwat in the valley of River Soan in the Potwar Plateau has reported the earliest pebble tools dating back to 2 million years. Pebble tools belonging to later dates are found from various other regions such as Jhelum basin (Dina and Jalalpur), the river terraces of Beas and Banganga (Himachal Pradesh) and Ladakh and Pahalgaon in Kashmir Valley. In Sind, Sukkur-Rohri hills have reported Acheulian tools, while Sanghao Cave near Peshawar has yielded evidence of Middle and Upper Palaeolithic occupation.

In Rajasthan, the evidence of Palaeolithic Cultures comes from both Marwar and Mewar — one to the west of the Aravallis and the other to its east. An important place in this state is Didwana (Distt. Nagaur) where a nearby site of Singhi Talav contains successive layers of Lower to Upper Palaeolithic material.

In Western India, the tools made on agate and jasper have been reported from various sites in South Gujarat, Saurashtra and Kutch.

In Maharastra, the most important sites are those of Nevasa, on a stream called Pravara (a tributary of Godavari) and Patne (Distt. Jalagaon) in the Tapti river system. Patne reveals an evolution of stone culture from the Middle Palaeolithic to the Mesolithic period. Among Upper Palaeolithic remains found here is a disc-bead made of a fragment of an ostrich egg-shell.

In Madhya Pradesh, the rock shelters at Bhimbetka (near Bhopal) and Adamgarh (Distt. Hoshangabad) have yielded evidence of Prehistoric occupation from Early Palaeolithic to the Mesolithic period. These rock shelters also contain a good number of rock-paintings, generally considered to be of the Mesolithic period, though some of them might belong to the Upper Palaeolithic phase. The site of Baghor in Sidhi district has also reported Upper Palaeolithic and Mesolithic tools.

In U.P., Palaeolithic remains have been discovered from various places but most prominently from the Belan Valley, the region broadly from Allahabad to Varanasi. It has revealed a complete sequence of the Stone Age Cultures from the Lower Palaeolithic to the Neolithic, extending even to the later periods. The site of Chopani Mando, 77 km from Allahabad, too has reported artifacts of the period from the Upper Palaeolithic to the Neolithic.

Towards the east, Assam and the neighbouring areas including Meghalaya (Garo Hills) contain some Prehistoric artifacts but, as Chakrabarti [1999: 73] argues, "more positive reports" are needed before they are included in the Palaeolithic distribution map of the subcontinent. In the region of Bengal, Palaeolithic tools occur in Birbhum, Burdwan, Purulia and Midnapore regions. Orissa is also rich in Palaeolithic material and it is mainly recovered from the districts of Mayurbhanj (where Kuliana is an important site), Sundargarh, Sambalpur and Bolangi. In Jharkhand, the districts of Singhbhum and Hazaribagh have yielded Palaeolithic artifacts. An important site in Bihar is Paisara (Distt. Munger) where Acheulian working floors of a factory site containing finished and semi-finished tools have been recovered.

In penisular India, Andhra Pradesh is rich in Palaeolithic material, and it is reported mainly from the districts of

Kurnool, Chittoor and Nalagonda. In Kurnool region, an important habitation site is the Muchchatha Chintamani Gavi cave which has revealed not only the earliest bone tools but also the earliest trace of hearth-fire in India [Chakrabarti: 1999: 79].

In Karnataka, the Malaprabha — Ghataprabha region, a tributary system of the river Krishna, contains a number of Palaeolithic sites such as Hunsgi (Distt. Gulbarga) and Kovalli and Anangwadi (both in Distt. Bijapur). The site of Kovalli is considered to have been an open air "factory-site" [Ghosh: 1989: Vol II, 239].

In north Tamil Nadu, Attirampakkam (Distt. Chingleput) is one of the key sites of the south Indian or the "Madrasian" Lower Palaeolithic industry.

The wide spread of Palaeolithic settlements clearly indicates that early man in India had adapted himself to a variety of eco-zones and that the Palaeolithic culture in India was not an isolated or a local phenomenon.

Settlement and Subsistence Pattern

The concept of settlement pattern was first used in archaeology by the American scholar G.R. Willey (1953) in his study on Prehistoric settlements in Perk, South America. It takes into consideration not only the spatial distribution of sites but also focuses on the factors behind the location of sites and the efforts made by man to exploit the immediate neighbourhood for food resources and raw material.

An analysis of the Palaeolithic sites in India indicates that human ancestors generally lived in open-air sites or in rock or cave shelters, wherever possible. The latter are few in number and are mostly located in Madhya Pradesh (Bhimbetka and

Adamgarh area). The sites were mostly close to the higher river banks or the hill terraces and their location was governed by the consideration of easy availability of perennial water, enough plant and animal food and the raw material for making tools.

These settlements were basically temporary camping sites or seasonal camps where hunter-gatherers returned after moving out for food for a short while. The rock shelters at Bhimbetka and other places, according to V.N. Misra, appear to have been occupied only during monsoons and the winter seasons, and in summer months human groups preferred to camp in the open. It is pointed out that these people lived in a group of 20 or 25 (called band) and their movement was determined by the seasonal availability of food resources not far away from their base near a hill or the water source. Vita-Finzi and Higgs [1970] in their studies on the Prehistoric economy of the Palestine region propounded the concept of "Site Catchment Analysis" and argued that early humans could not have walked more than 10 km away from their base to exploit food and mineral resources. K. Paddaya [1982] confirming this assertion points out that the sites in the Hunsgi region (Karnataka) did have their resources within a radius of 10 km.

There is little evidence available about the dwellings or habitation structures of the early humans in Palaeolithic period. However, the indications of alignment of slab-like pieces or granite blocks at Hunsgi (Karnataka) and of post-holes at Paisara (Munger, Bihar), according to some scholars, suggest the use of some thatched roof-like structures. There is also no direct evidence of their subsistence practices but there is no doubt that animal food acquired through hunting or scavenging formed the chief item of their diet, though some plant food also must have been a part of it.

The craft activity of the Palaeolithic people is demonstrated in the growing skill in making finer and sharper stone tools and in the selection of better and more compatible raw material. Some of the sites such as Hunsgi and Kovali in Karnataka, Paisara in Bihar, and many others in the Belan valley have been termed as "factory sites" as they have yielded not only finished tools but also flakes and unfinished tools. It is possible that these places supplied finished tools to other regions, indicating some inter-regional contact, the exact nature of which cannot be determined. However, similarity in tool-making techniques over a far-flung area in the Indian sub-continent may suggest a fair amount of socio-economic communicability among different regions.

As regard the religious beliefs and practices of the Palaeolithic people, some efforts have been made to draw conjectural inferences on the basis of limited data. For example, in the Upper Palaeolithic layer at Baghor (Madhya Pradesh), there has been found a rubble-built platform with a triangular piece of natural stone in the centre. Some scholars, on the basis of its similarity with the present day local shrines in the region, identify it with a place where mother-goddess was worshipped. This contention, however, is not free from doubt. Similarly, a bone object belonging to the Upper Palaeolithic phase from Lohanda Nala (Allahabad) in the Belan Valley has been identified by G.R. Sharma as a figurine of a mother goddess, but Wakankar and Bednarik prefer to describe it as a harpoon.

As for their artistic activity, an important evidence of it comes from an engraved ostrich egg-shell fragment with criss-cross designs within horizontal lines found at Patne, Maharashtra. Besides, the earliest layers of rock-paintings at Bhimbetka, according to V.S. Wakankar, might have belonged to the Upper Palaeolithic Age.

Conclusion

In short, in the Palaeolithic period, which forms the longest phase of human history, man lived by hunting animals and gathering wild fruits. He inhabitated the area close to river banks and hilly terraces where there were enough food and mineral resources for his requirements. His survival depended upon his efficiency to make stone tools which, with experience, became sharper and more handy. The tool-making required a great deal of knowledge and expertise not only in selecting a suitable raw material but also in technique to turn it into a desired shape. The gradual refinement in tool-types represented the cultural growth of Palaeolithic man and set the stage for further progress in the next phase called the Mesolithic phase.

4

Mesolithic Cultures

Introduction

THE Mesolithic or the Middle Stone Age Cultures represent a phase of transition from the preceding hunting and food-gathering stage of the Palaeolithic period to that of farming and herding in the succeeding Neolithic period. The earliest evidence of the presence of Mesolithic man in India was noted as early as 1867-68 by A.C.L. Carlyle who had discovered a large number of microliths in the caves and rock shelters in the Kaimur range (Mirzapur district of Uttar Pradesh). But there had been no significant progress in our knowledge of Mesolithic period until H.D. Sankalia undertook excavations in 1950s at Langhnaj and other places in Gujarat. Sometimes Mesolithic period is treated as a later part of the Palaeolithic Age (Epipalaeolithic) but in Indian context the term Mesolithic has come to be accepted as a separate phase of the Prehistoric culture. It was marked by a significant improvement in tool technology and life pattern though some of the earlier traditions continued to exist.

Salient Features

The Mesolithic period coincides with the beginning of the Holocene age, around 10,000 BP or 8,000 BC. This age, as mentioned earlier, witnessed a change in climate from cold and arid to warm and wet on account of the gradual recession of the glaciers. This change led to the melting of snow and the formation of rivers resulting in the growth of forests and vegetation. Though our knowledge on palaeoclimatic variation in India is still limited, the study of pollens and sediments by Gurdip Singh and his associates in Rajasthan and the geological studies by Williams and Clark in eastern Madhya Pradesh indicate that there was a marked increase in rainfall in these regions at the beginning of the Holocene age [Chakrabarti: 1999: 95-8]. The change in climate naturally affected both flora and fauna. The giant animals that roamed the surface of earth in the "Ice-age" gradually vanished and these were replaced with swifter and smaller animals such as various species of deer, cattle, sheep, goat, etc. The fish also became more abundant. The new environment thus created conditions for the availability of new resources, and in order to exploit them more effectively, it became essential for the Mesolithic man to make necessary modifications in his tool-types. The characteristic tool of the Mesolithic period was "microlith," a small-sized stone tool of different shapes which could be hafted on a wooden or a bone handle to make a "composite tool" or a weapon such as spear, arrow, sickle or saw. These tools could be employed more profitably for hunting as well as for collecting vegetal food.

An important feature of the Mesolithic period was the significant growth in population and the change in demographic profile. It, according to V.N. Misra [2002: 114] is evident from the fact that sites of this period are much larger in number than those of the preceding Palaeolithic stage. At Bhimbetka, for example, while the evidence of Palaeolithic occupation has been found in only a few shelters, that of the Mesolithic period is found in almost every shelter. Further, it is during this period that the humans extended their habitat into the alluvial plains of the Ganga in the south-central Uttar Pradesh. Interestingly, two of the sites, viz., Chopani Mando and Sarai Nahar Rai (Allahabad-Pratapgarh area) in this region are situated as far as eighty km from the nearest source of basic raw material of stone. It has led V.N. Misra to argue that it was the growth in population which must have forced these human groups to settle in far off areas where they had to import stone for their requirements. U.C. Chattopadyaya [1996] is of the opinion that these people of the Gangetic valley might have been producing, on account of better environment, meat in excess of their requirement and were thus in a position to exchange it with the raw material for their stone tools from the neighbouring regions.

It is suggested that greater availability of food and better health of the people were probably the main factors which led to decrease in mortality rate and the increase in population. While better rainfall in Holocene age contributed to greater plant growth as well as increase in fish and animal population, the use of microliths as arrows or spear-heads greatly improved the hunting efficiency of the Mesolithic man. The evidence of querns and mullers which appear for the first time in this period further confirms that plant food was supplementing the animal diet. Thus, assured of better food supply, the Mesolithic man led a healthier and a longer life.

The Mesolithic period is also significant because the evidence of burials or the ritual of intentional disposal of the dead appears for the first time during this period. The grave goods such as bone beads, rings, etc., put along with the dead in some of the graves, are greatly helpful in giving us an insight into the beliefs, rituals and the craft activities of the Mesolithic man. Finally, the earliest rock paintings in India belong primarily to this period. They throw valuable light not only on the aesthetic sense and artistic taste of the Mesolithic people but also enable us to reconstruct their socio-economic behaviour.

Chronologically, Indian Mesolithic cultures are normally placed between 8,000 BC to 5,000-4,000 BC. But on the basis of a copper knife reported from Langhnaj (Gujarat) and the C_{14} dates received from various other sites, it is assigned to a broad time-span ranging from 8,000 BC - 2,000 BC, surviving well into the Neolithic and Chalcolithic phases [Possehl and Rissman: 1992: 465].

Regional Distribution

In the last five decades, a large number of Mesolithic sites have been discovered and excavated **(see Figure 4)**. They are located all over the country, except in the regions of north-east India and the delta of Bengal in the east, the Punjab plains and the Gangetic plain beyond Allahabad in the north, and Kerala in the south. It is believed that the absence of microlithic sites in these areas was due either to the lack of stone for making tools or to the heavy rainfall and dense vegetation.

However, their density is far greater in some areas like Marwar and Mewar in Rajasthan, north Gujarat and the alluvial plain of the Ganga in south-central U.P., i.e. Allahabad — Mirzapur area. Among the important microlithic sites reference may be made to Bagor (25 km west of Distt. Bhilwara) and Tilwara (Distt. Barmer, on the left bank of the river Luni) in Rajasthan; Langhnaj (Distt. Mehsana) in Gujarat; Bhimbetka (45 km south of Bhopal), Adamgarh (Distt. Hoshangabad) and Baghor (Distt. Sidhi) in Madhya Pradesh; Chopani Mando (77 km south-east of Allahabad in the Belan Valley), Sarai Nahar Rai (Distt. Pratapgarh), Mahadaha, Damdama, Lekhania (Distt.

Mirzapur) — all in UP; Birbhanpur (Distt. Burdwan) in West Bengal; Kuchai (Distt. Mayurbhanj) in Orissa; Sanaganakallu (Distt. Bellary) in Karnataka; and Tuticorin in south Tamil

PRINCIPAL SITES OF MESOLITHIC CULTURES AND ROCK PAINTINGS

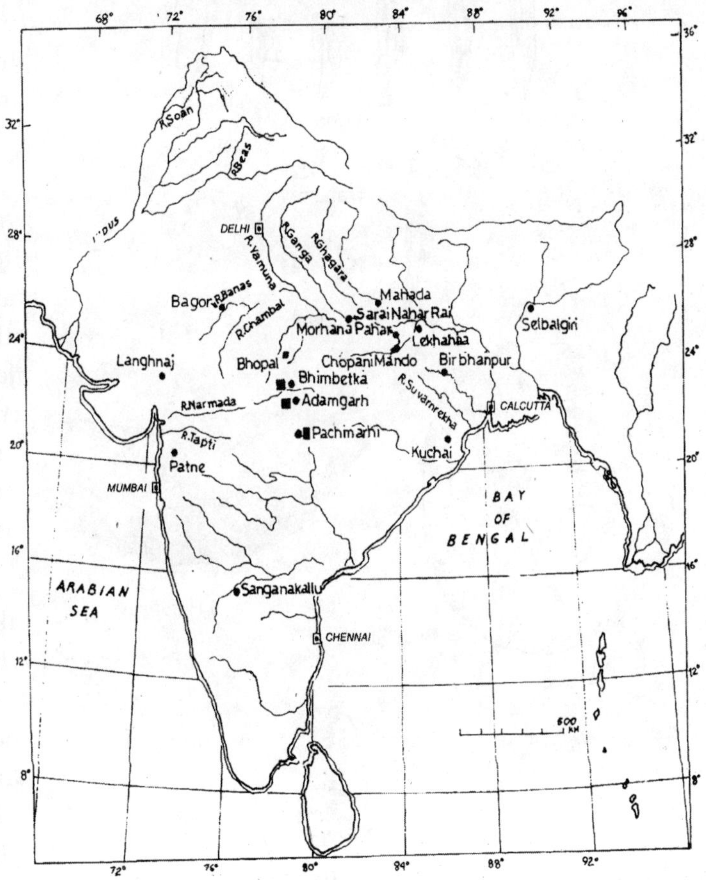

● MESOLITHIC CULTURES

■ ROCK PAINTINGS

Fig. 4

Nadu. In the last region, the microliths have been reported in the red sand dunes which are locally known as *teris*, and thus this industry is known as teri industry.

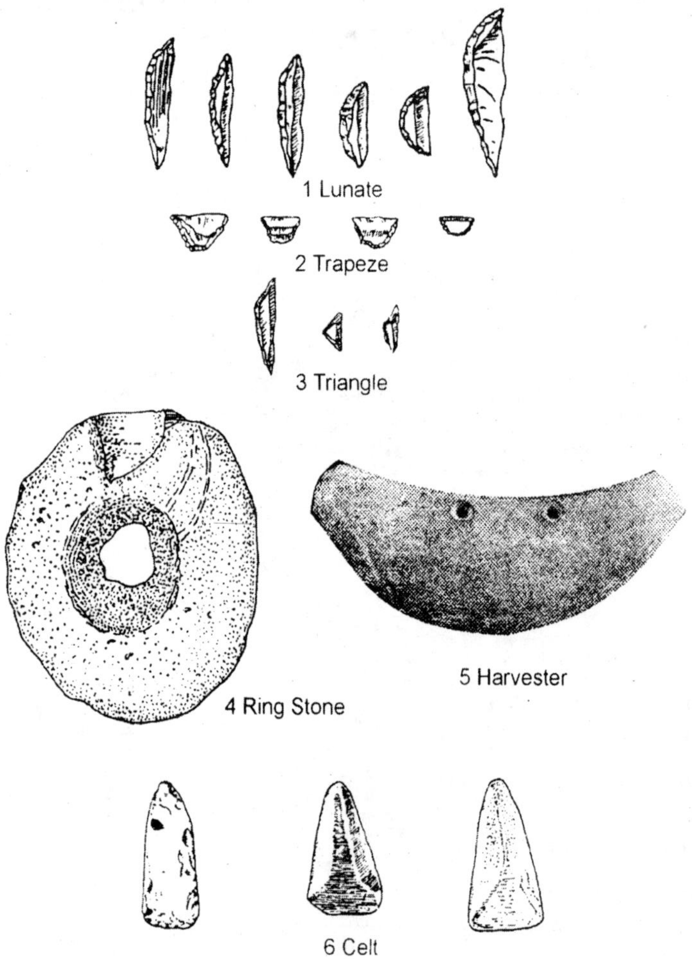

Some Mesolithic and Neolithic Tools —
1 to 3 are Mesolithic and 4 to 6 are Neolithic

Fig. 5

An overview of the spread of microlithic sites will indicate that the Mesolithic communities were settled in a variety of environments which included sand dunes, rock shelters and also the alluvial plains of the mid-Ganga valley where they had enough water, food resources and raw material for tools. They also extended their habitat into areas previously either totally unoccupied or occupied only sparsely.

Tools and Technologies

The chief feature of the Mesolithic period was the use of a large number of microliths or blades and bladelets, produced from a well-prepared cylindrical or rectangular core by pressure flaking with the help of a bone or a wooden hammer **(see Figure 5)**. It represents a technological improvement on the earlier tool-making techniques which were based on direct or indirect hitting or flaking. There was also a change in the use of raw material in most areas. Except in parts of south India where fine type of quartzite was available, in all other areas people switched over to chert, chalcedony, agate, jasper and other fine-grained stones which occur in the form of small nodules.

The pressure technique economised the precious raw material and produced more blades in lesser time. The blades thus produced were further retouched or trimmed on one or more edges to produce a variety of "**geometric**" type microliths in the shape of triangles, lunates or crescents, trapezes, etc. These tools, the size of which varied from less than one centimetre to five centimetres could be hafted on bone or wooden handles with natural gum to produce a "composite tool" or a weapon such as arrow or spear. Many contemporary paintings at Bhimbetka and other places reveal the use of such arrowheads and spearheads. The microliths could also be arranged in a linear series to provide a serrated edge to make a composite tool to serve as a saw or a sickle. The main advantage of these 'composite tools' was that being made of a number of microliths, if one of the teeth broke down, it could easily be replaced without having to discard the whole tool as was the case with a single-piece tool of earlier times.

Besides microliths, small non-geometric tools also formed a part of the Mesolithic tool-kit. These were usually made on flakes by secondary trimming along the margin. This group of tools included various types of scrapers, burins, etc. The site of Mohrana Pahar in Mirzapur (U.P.) reveals a gradual process of evolution of lithic tools from non-geometric to geometric ones. Large flake-tools like chopper and chopping tools are by and large absent, though some examples of these could be found in Tamil Nadu region.

Apart from flake stone tools, the Mesolithic people also used other tools which included hammer stone, perforated discs or ring stones, querns and rubbers. The hammer-stone was used, besides other things, for splitting animal bones; the function of the ring stone appears to have been to serve either as a mace-head or a weight for a digging stick with the help a wooden handle. Querns and rubbers must have been used for processing both plant and animal food. It may be mentioned that some of the sites such as Langhnaj and Bagor have also reported hand-made pottery. The sherds are, however, very small and generally shapeless, and there is no evidence that these vessels were used for cooking [Varma: 1985: 32-3].

There is also evidence of the use of tools and ornaments made of bone and antler by the Mesolithic people. These include arrowheads, blades, knives and also rings which have been found worn as earrings and necklaces in the burials. Such bone tools have been reported from Sarai Nahar Rai and

Mahadaha in the Gangetic Valley [V.N. Misra: 2002: 118]. (Antler is a solid bony horn shed by a male deer once a year. It grows back again next year).

Material Culture and Subsistence Pattern

Our knowledge on the dwellings and material culture of the Mesolithic people is quite limited. However, the excavations at certain sites such as Bagor, Tilwara, Sarai Nahar Rai, etc., have revealed that they lived in semi-permanent hut-like structures having wattle and daub walls (walls made of tree twigs and branches plastered with mud) and paved floors. The post-holes found on the periphery of hutments suggest the presence of a roof-like structure for protection. In central India, these people preferred to stay in readily available rock shelters.

The animal bones and stone tools found at various sites form the chief evidence of the subsistence pattern of the Mesolithic people. This direct evidence is supplemented by the depiction of scenes of hunting, fishing, trapping of mice and plant food collection in the contemporary rock paintings. The animal species identified on the basis of bones include both domesticated and non-domesticated varieties such as wild bear, wolf, rhino, cattle, goat, sheep, etc. At Bagor, a paved floor littered with bones has been identified by V.N. Misra as a place for butchering animals or a slaughter house. The bones found in broken, split open and charred conditions indicate that the meat was cooked or roasted on open fire [V.N. Misra: 2002: 119]. At Bagor and Adamgarh there is evidence of domestication of cattle, sheep and goat. Allchin [1997: 92] however doubts the domestication of cattle but agrees that sheep/goat were "certainly domesticated" in this period. Anyway, the Mesolithic period presents the earliest evidence of the domestication of animals in India, and suggests that the early humans had now started combining hunting with stock-breeding.

The earliest evidence of human burials in India also comes from the Mesolithic period, and these are reported from various sites such as Langhnaj, Bagor and Sarai Nahar Rai. The deads were buried inside the habitational area, and the most common form of burial was the extended burial, a body lying on the back with face upward. There are, however, some variations too. Sometimes, the dead were buried in a flexed position with arms and legs folded as if in a sleeping position. There is also evidence of secondary or fractional burials, having only a few bones. It is, however, not known whether different types of burials represent different ethnic groups or communities living together.

Generally, one grave contained a single individual, but sometimes two, three and even more bodies were placed in one and the same grave. At Sarai Nahar Rai, a grave contains four individuals in two pairs of a male and a female each, the male being placed on the right of the female. It, according to R.K. Varma [1985: 34], makes one ponder whether the concept of a family in the form of a wife-husband unit had already evolved during the Mesolithic period. Anyhow, the meticulous way in which the burials were made and the way in which the dead bodies and grave goods were placed clearly indicate the performance of some ritual at the time of death and the emergence of belief in life after death.

The grave goods obtained from the graves give us an important insight into the material culture of the Mesolithic people. These goods include microliths and bone ornaments. At Mahadaha, one skeleton is wearing an earring along with a necklace of beads made of antler bone. Mahadaha has in fact been identified as a place where bone tools and ornaments were manufactured [Allchin: 1997: 92]. Beads of semi-precious stones such as jasper and agate have been reported from Bagor, Bhimbetka and Adamgarh [V.D. Misra: 1999: 238]. It appears that the ornaments were probably used by the people of higher status and may indicate the beginning of some sort of social division or stratification in the Mesolithic period, the nature and characteristics of which are not clear. This period, anyway, reveals the earliest use of ornaments and sheds enough light on the craft activity and aesthetic sensibility of the Mesolithic people.

Conclusion

In short, the Mesolithic phase of Prehistory was characterised by the introduction of new tool technology in the form of microliths and 'composite tools' as well as by some progress towards the domestication of animals and plant collection. The evidence from Langhnaj (Gujarat), Bagor (Rajasthan) and Adamgarh (Madhya Pradesh) which have reported the bones of sheep and cattle indicates that initial microlithic phase of hunting economy was being gradually replaced by cattle-herding. The beads of shell in the skeletal remains from Langhnaj, which must have been imported from distant sea, and the microlithic tools from Sarai Nahar Rai (U.P.), a site which is away from the source of raw material, suggest that some sort of exchange system or trade mechanism had grown among the Mesolithic societies. The existence of hut-like structures and the food-processing artifacts such as querns and mullers indicate the beginning of a quasi-sedentary or semi-settled life. Though it is not possible at the present stage to define how settled was their life, it may be surmised that wherever food and water was available all the year round, the Mesolithic people might have lived permanently. Thus, the life pattern in the Mesolithic period suggests that man was already on the threshold of the Neolithic phase — a phase dominated by the beginning of farming activities, cattle-herding and settled life.

Rock Art

The Rock art represents the earliest evidence of aesthetic taste and expression of man in India and constitutes a valuable source of visual information on the lives, beliefs and preoccupations of the Prehistoric hunting and gathering communities. It includes paintings as well as engravings made on the rock surface.

The rock paintings in India were first discovered by A. Carlleyle on the walls and ceilings of rock shelters in Distt. Mirzapur (U.P.) in 1867-68. Since then more than one hundred and fifty rock art sites have come to light. These are spread all over the Indian subcontinent from the Himalayas in the north to Kerala in the south. Their major concentration, however, is in Madhya Pradesh and central U.P. (south Mirzapur region). Bhimbetka with around six hundred painted rocks within an area of ten sq. km is the largest centre of rock paintings in the country. As for the line drawings, the evidence has come from the regions which include Chilas in Gilgit-Karakorum area, Leh in Ladakh, Burzahom in Kashmir, and Koppugallu and Sanaganakallu in Karnataka. It may be pointed out that Rock art sites, though these are distributed all over the country and exhibit regional variations, reflect broad uniformity in terms of subject matter, technique, style and the pigments used.

Almost three-fourths of the total rock art sites in India are situated in the sand-stone hills of the Vindhyas in central India. The reason for this is that sand-stone being soft is susceptible to erosion as a natural process under the effect of weather. Therefore, sometimes massive rock pieces when thus eroded slip and come to rest against other rocks, thereby forming a natural rock shelter. Besides, this area contains thick forests with plentiful animals and enough supply of water from nearby springs. It thus provided the early man with an ideal place for inhabitation.

The rock art in India covers a fairly long period and depicts different themes and styles. Efforts have been made to fix its **chronology** on the basis of subject matter, style and the nature of stone tools discovered at the site. Sometimes, the later artists have drawn their own paintings without caring to erase the earlier ones. These superimpositions also have been helpful in establishing the relative chronology of the paintings. V.S. Wakankar believes that the paintings at Bhimbetka executed in green pigment appear to have been the earliest and may be dated to the Upper Palaeolithic period. But, other scholars such as Mathpal, Allchin and Chakrabarti argue that changing themes and styles rather than pigments of the paintings may be a better method of fixing the chronology, and suggest that the paintings which depict only animals or men in hunting and gathering activities may be treated as the earliest and should be assigned to the Mesolithic period going back to 8,000 BC. However, as these paintings come to us in a mature and developed form, an older tradition of art going back in time to Upper Palaeolithic period cannot be ruled out.

On the basis of style and **subject matter**, Indian rock art has been divided broadly into three phases: (i) prehistoric, Upper Palaeolithic/Mesolithic phase, dominated by wild animals and hunting gathering scenes; (ii) transitional, Neolithic-Chalcolithic phase, depicting domesticated animals and agriculture related activities; and (iii) historical, going up to the Gupta period, portraying warriors carrying swords and spears seated on horses and elephants.

As far as the Prehistoric paintings are concerned, the cave artists used the colours prepared out of the locally available minerals. The most common colour is red derived from ochre. It is found in various shades such as vermilion, orange and light red. The second common colour is white, derived from lime. Green and yellow colours have also been used but rarely.

It appears that mineral nodules were diluted with water and then mixed with animal fat and plant-juice or glue to make pigments. Paintings are basically monochromic and are drawn on natural rock surface without any preparation of background such as smoothening or plastering. The brushes made of twig or animal hair were used.

The subject matter of the Prehistoric art consists primarily of wild animals and hunting scenes. A great variety of animals are depicted, and these include deer, nilgai, wild buffalo, boar, rhino, tiger, etc. At some sites such as Lakhajuar near Bhimbetka, fish is a common theme. The representation of birds and plants is insignificant suggesting absence of agricultural activities.

The animals are portrayed in different postures and moods such as standing, moving, running and grazing. They are realistically drawn and their size varies from a few centimeters to life size. The outlines of their bodies are often filled and decorated with various geometric patterns such as straight or wavy lines or criss-cross patterns.

It is pointed out that in the earliest paintings animals were shown alone but gradually human figures came to be associated with them. The humans are mostly drawn in a conventional manner, and are stick-shaped and disproportionately long. The hunting scenes which are quite common usually depict an individual hunter hunting one or more animals or a group of hunters hunting a large herd. The men are shown carrying sticks, spears, bows and arrows. In several cases, the arrows and spears are barbed or tipped with what appears to be microlithic chips. The positioning of hunters around the animal indicates that hunting was done in a planned manner. In one scene from Bhimbetka, several animals are shown falling down a steep cliff suggesting they were chased down to meet their end. There are also scenes of hunting big animals such as elephants and rhinos. In one hunting scene, a hunter is tossed up in the air by the horn of the rhino indicating the danger which such activities posed. The scenes portraying the use of stick to draw the rats out of the hole as well as of fishing are also recorded. Other subsistence activities depicted are the collection of honey and fruits by men and women climbing the tree **(see Figures 6 & 7)**.

Family groups and their related activities too form a theme of some of the rock paintings. At Bhimbetka, there is a pathetic scene of a child burial mourned by males and females. There is also a picture which depicts a man, a woman and a child in a house eating together. It may suggest the beginning of a family group, the exact nature of which one cannot be ascertained. There are scenes of women either in higher stage of pregnancy or nursing children or indulging in sexual activity. At Kupgallu (Karnataka) there is a scene showing abduction of females by excited males. It can't be ascertained whether this depiction refers to some war or a tribal ritual connected with marriage system.

It may be pointed out that the Prehistoric paintings normally project males as more conquering and domineering

1. Dynamic dancing human figures painted in green colour:

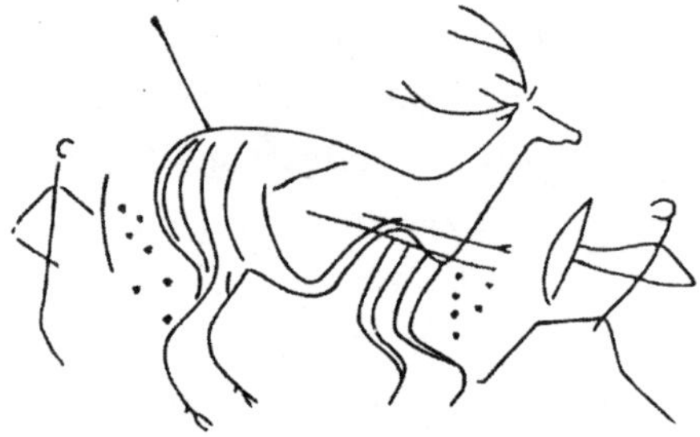

2. Hunting scene.

3. Hunter carrying a net filled with hunt.

Fig. 6

than women. Women are no doubt depicted in hunting scenes but they are never shown as part of the active hunting group, and stand aloof with digging sticks. They are normally portrayed as involved in less hazardous activities such as vegetable and food gathering or fish and rat catching or working on querns and rubber stones. Thus, as Neumayer [1993: 76, 100] observes, the Indian Prehistoric rock paintings clearly depict a sex-defined or "sex-based division of labour."

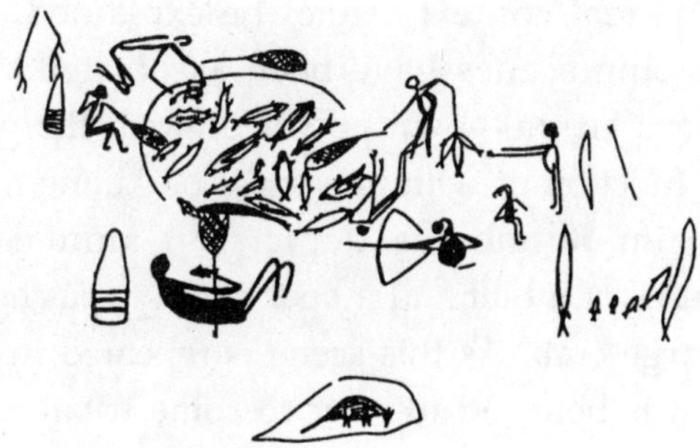

4. Fishing scene.

5. Women engaged in catching cats.

6. A family in a hut-like structure.

7. Burial scene.

Fig. 7

Some of the rock paintings seem to refer to the religious beliefs and superstitions of the Prehistoric man. However, it is difficult to assess their actual significance. There are, for example, paintings in which hunters are shown wearing masks. This depiction may be associated with some ritual or occult practice, but its real context cannot be explained. Similarly, the group-dancing scenes have been associated with some ritual to appease an unknown power or with the celebration of some social function or with happiness on killing a big game. A painting from Bhimbetka depicts an animal with the combined features of a bull and a boar angrily chasing a human figure and a large crab. As this scene is repeated in two other rock-shelters, it is believed to refer to some tribal mythology.

What was the main **motive** or purpose behind the rock art of Prehistoric man, we do not know but it is certain that it was not inspired just by the desire to decorate rock shelters and did carry some silent message. While some scholars believe that these paintings may have been the medium to express and explain the thoughts and planning, perhaps on hunting tactics, before the advent of the language, many others relate them with Prehistoric man's magico-ritual urge and suggest that painted rock shelters might have been the places for performing sacred rituals. The latter presumption is based on the fact that the most profusely painted shelters have little or no indication of human occupation as they contain no evidence of smoke or other organic material, whereas shelters indicating long occupation are poor in paintings [Mathpal: 1984]. The ritual function of the painted shelters is also attested from the ethnological studies on the life of the Australian aborigines.

In short, the Prehistoric art belonging to the Mesolithic period adds a great deal to our knowledge on the hunting and gathering techniques of the early cave-dwellers. The paintings depicting masked hunters, pregnant women, conjugal life, mourning and dancing scenes give us an insight into their socio-religious behaviour not known from other archaeological data.

5

Neolithic Cultures

Introduction

THE Neolithic Cultures constitute the concluding phase of the Stone age. These were marked by the use of ground and polished tools and the pottery — the features which set them apart from the preceding Palaeolithic and Mesolithic Cultures. The term "Neolithic" was first used by the Danish prehistorian, Thomsen, in the nineteenth century to denote the stage of technological progress achieved by early man. But it was Gordon Childe who highlighted the true socio-economic significance of these cultures by associating them with the emergence of the practice of plant cultivation and animal domestication leading to the growth of farming communities and a settled village life. He used the term "**Neolithic Revolution**" to emphasize this progress. He also argued that farming was first invented in a single "nuclear region" in Mesopotamia or Near-East from where it diffused and spread to India and other parts of the world.

The hypothesis of Gordon Childe, however, is not substantiated by modern research. The prehistorians though by and large agree that new subsistence economy based on farming and stock-raising was a turning point in the development of human civilization, they disapprove the use of the term 'Revolution.' According to them, the term

'Revolution' conveys the idea of some sudden or abrupt change whereas the transition to Neolithic life was a part of a long drawn process, the beginnings of which could be noticed in the earlier Palaeolithic and the Mesolithic phases. Childe had initially put forward his idea in the book, *New Light on Most Ancient* (1934: 296-97), but later in *The Prehistory of European Society* (1958: 35), while he retained the term "Neolithic Revolution," he conceded that it did not imply a single catastrophic change and that this change was "the culmination of a gradual progress, begun centuries earlier." It is now generally agreed that progress in Neolithic period may be treated more as a "transformation" or "evolution" rather than a "revolution." Childe had also erred when he argued for the diffusion of agricultural activities from Middle-East to other parts of the world. Modern researches indicate that wherever geographical factors permitted, the Neolithic people took up farming activities in a normal way and, therefore, there could be not one but several regions in the world where farming communities might have developed independently. In fact, the shift from earlier hunting and gathering society to food-producing farming communities may be viewed in the context of several factors including the change in climate which became more conducive to plant growth with the onset of the Holocene Age, technological experience of the earlier societies and the increase in population.

Characteristic Features

Technologically speaking, the Neolithic period was characterized by the ground and polished tools having smooth and round surface for better cutting edge. These tools mark an improvement on earlier ones which once damaged had to be discarded, but now after grinding them they could once more be rendered serviceable. Thus, with the growth of grinding technique, there was an economy of effort as well as of the raw material. The chief tool-type of this age is designated by the common term 'celt' which is basically an axe or adze. It might have been used to clear the area of wild vegetation and make it fit for cultivation.

Pottery, though initially rough and hand-made, also appears for the first time in this age. It was used not only for cooking but also for storing the food-grains. The growing reliance on cereals is reflected in the discovery of a large number of stone querns, pestles and ring-stones (the flat stone slabs with a hole in the centre to fix a rod or a shaft) which could be used for crushing or pounding an agricultural produce **(see Figure 5)**. As the cultivation of cereals and the domestication of animals provided a greater certainty of food supply, the growth of larger communities with settled life became possible. The man started living in wattle-and-daub houses, the houses made of twigs and sticks plastered with mud. There also developed certain religious beliefs and practices as is evident from the planned burials belonging to the period. The presence of beads and ornaments of sea-shell and lapis lazuli and other semi-precious stones at certain sites, for example at Mehrgarh, suggest that these products or the raw materials for them were brought from their resource areas far away in distance. It indicates the existence of some sort of rudimentary exchange system. In other words, Neolithic period was marked by qualitative changes not only in tool-making techniques but also in the socio-economic spheres of humankind.

Chronological and Distributional Pattern

A Neolithic celt in India was found as early as 1842 by Le Mesurie in the Raichur district of Karnataka, and later by John

Lubbock in 1867 in the Brahmaputra valley of Upper Assam. Today, as a result of vast explorations and excavations, the

PRINCIPAL SITES OF NEOLITHIC CULTURES

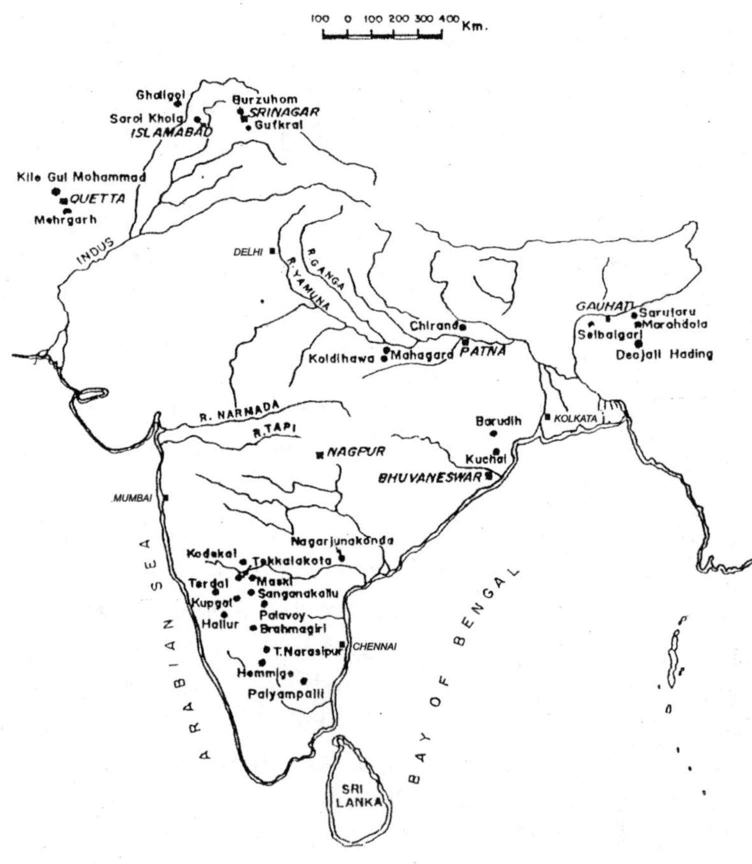

Fig. 8

evidence of the spread of Neolithic Cultures in India comes from as many as six different geographical regions, each with its own distinctive features and chronological time-span **(see Figure 8)**. These regions are, (i) North-western, i.e.,

Baluchistan and its adjoining area in Pakistan (7th to mid 4th millennium BC), (ii) Northern, i.e., Kashmir Valley (2500 BC – 1500 BC), (iii) Central India, i.e., Vindhyan region, south of Allahabad (4000 BC – 1200 BC), (iv) mid-Gangetic basin, i.e., eastern U.P. and Bihar (2000 BC – 1500 BC), (v) Eastern India, i.e., Bengal, Orissa and Assam, (vi) Peninsular or south India, i.e., Andhra, Karnataka and Tamil Nadu (2500 BC – 1500 BC).

An overview of the above time-frame will indicate that the Neolithic phase in India did not develop everywhere at the same time nor did it end simultaneously. In fact, there were many Neolithic cultures which were co-existing with the copper-using urban Harappan Civilization (2600 BC – 1900 BC). These cultures, besides having different time-frame, exhibit some regional variations too. For example, in the north-east region, Neolithic tools have been found but there is no evidence of plant cultivation. Similarly, while most of the Neolithic Cultures evolved out of the preceding Mesolithic Cultures, no such evidence is reported from Kashmir Valley. In the matter of food production too it is noticed that while wheat and barley were predominant cereals at Mehrgarh in Baluchistan, it was rice that formed an important crop in the central region around Allahabad. In south India the Neolithic Cultures were characterised by millet and ragi cultivation with "ashmounds" as their the chief characteristic features.

The variations in different Neolithic Cultures as classified above suggest that each of them was conditioned by its own geographical setting, and therefore they need to be studied separately. It must be mentioned that with all their diversity in terms of time, space and local features, the net result of the Neolithic Cultures wherever they developed, was broadly the same, i.e., the rise of farming and sedentary village communities. The large spread of the Neolithic Cultures also indicates that farming activity in India was not an isolated feature but was an all-India phenomenon.

NORTH-WEST INDIA

The earliest evidence of the Neolithic Culture marked by growth of farming and animal husbandry in the Indian subcontinent is obtained from the regions of Baluchistan and the North-West Frontier Province of Pakistan. The relevant sites include Mehrgarh, Killi Gul Muhammad, Rana Gundai in Baluchistan; and Gumla, Rehman Dheri, Tarakai Qila and Sarai Khola in NWFP. **Mehrgarh** is the chief representative site where the excavations carried out by J.F. Jarrige and others in 1970s and 1980s revealed a continuity in the growth and consolidation of village life which gradually merged with the urbanised Harappan culture later. Mehrgarh presents a picture of continuous growth dating back from the seventh millennium BC to the third millennium BC. A transition from aceramic (pre-pottery) phase to hand-made and wheel-turned pottery is also clearly marked here.

Mehrgarh is situated on the banks of the River Bolan in Kachi plains, about 150 km south-east of Quetta in Baluchistan. Kachi plains lie in a semi-arid region where three environmental zones, viz., hills, plains and rivers, come together and make the region quite suitable for the development of farming economy. It is postulated by Jarrige that in the Late Paleistocene period, local hunters and gatherers fed themselves by collecting wild grass and fruits in the foot-hills and by hunting on open slopes or in the plains near watering points, but gradually they took up cereal cultivation as an important means of subsistence. It is now generally believed [Possehl : 1999: 405; D.P. Agrawal : 2002: 166] that the process of farming and animal domestication in the region was a local phenomenon rather than an import from outside.

Chronologically, the Neolithic cultures of north-western region are assigned to a time bracket from the seventh millennium BC to the mid fourth millennium BC, and are divided into a number of periods and sub-periods to mark out the change and continuity in the subsistence patterns. Though on account of a number of overlapping dates, the time-frame for each phase is not particularly clear, the sequence of Neolithic culture at Mehrgarh may be divided broadly in three periods, viz., Period I from 7000 – 5500 BC; Period II, from 5500 BC – 4500 BC; Period III, 4500 BC – 3500 BC. Among other sites which reveal the evidence of Neolithic Culture are Killi Gul Muhammad, dating from 5500 BC; Rana Gundai from 4500 BC; and Damb Saadat from 3000 BC.

The earliest phase at Mehrgarh, Pd. I (7000 BC – 5500 BC), was largely aceramic and was dominated by stone and bone tools. The stone tools included polished axes, chisels, querns and also microliths such as lunates and triangles. The bone tools comprised awls (pointed tool for making a hole), needles, etc. This period has also yielded the evidence of agriculture and domestication of animals. Though hunting continued to be a dominant occupation, the bones of cattle, sheep and goat indicate their domestication. There are also bones of water-buffalo which, according to some scholars, represent the earliest evidence of the domestication of this animal in South Asia. People lived in mud-brick houses which were small in the beginning but gradually became bigger. Some of the buildings have revealed small cell-like compartments suggesting that these might have been used for the storage of grains. The evidence of agriculture comes from the finds of charred seeds of wheat and barley, the latter being more prominent. The other plant-food which people consumed was the Indian jujube (ber) and dates. The craft activity in this period is reflected in the grave goods which include the microbeads of steatite, lapis lazuli and turquoise and also the rings and bangles of seashell. Since the raw material for these goods is not available in the immediate neighbourhood of Mehrgarh, it is obvious that lapis lazuli came from Afghanistan, turquoise from central Asia or north-east Iran, and seashell from the coastal area about five hundred kilometres away. This is a clear indication that the people of Mehrgarh even in Pd. I were not isolated to the world around and were involved in economic interaction with other contemporary cultures. It also indicates the emergence of craft activity and the gradual diversification of economic base. The use of ornaments by some persons may suggest the beginning of social stratification marked by rich and poor.

Pd. II (5500 BC – 4500 BC) was more or less the continuation of Pd. I as far as tool-types are concerned, but a special feature of this phase was the introduction of handmade pottery with no floral or faunal motif; the wheel-turned pottery begins to appear later in the phase. The mud-brick structures were now larger and they had facilities for storage of grains. A structure found at the site has been assumed to be a "granary." This assumption seems to be valid because besides a large number of seeds of barley and wheat, there have been found two "sickle" like tools, each consisting of three stone blade pieces set obliquely in a wooden handle. This is the earliest evidence of a 'composite tool' in India. It might have been used for agricultural activity. Another important discovery is that of a steatite workshop where raw materials for making beads as well as several finished bead pieces have been found. A large number of charred cotton seeds have also been found near this place. This constitutes the earliest evidence of cotton plantation in the world, and it may be fairly assumed that spinning and weaving might have begun in India as far back as the fifth millennium BC. There also occurs an elephant tusk bearing groove marks. This is again taken as the earliest evidence of ivory-working in the Indian subcontinent. Terracotta human figurines have also been found. Beads of lapis lazuli and turquoise continue to appear in the graves suggesting interaction with distant areas of their origin. The second phase of Mehrgarh has thus characterised by a greater diversification of the economic base.

Pd. III, begins with c. 4500 BC, and it witnesses a consolidation of agricultural and cattle-herding activities marked by surplus production. A number of collective graves which appear in this period may indicate an increase in population, probably on account of better and more assured food supply. A study of dental remains made by J.R. Lukacs and his associates suggests that the people in this period suffered from increasing dental problems such as dental caries and tooth-loss which may be on account of greater reliance on carbohydrated-cultivated food.

This period is associated with further growth in craft activities. The wheel-turned pottery with paintings depicting human and floral designs makes its appearance in this period. The waste material of carnelian, turquoise, shell, etc., found at the site indicates that crafts associated with these were a local feature. The traces of copper found in crucibles suggest that the people at Mehrgarh were also engaged in copper-smelting. According to D.K. Chakrabarti [1999: 125], this is the earliest evidence of copper smelting in the Indian subcontinent.

In short, Mehrgarh presents a picture of continuous growth of village life and the diversification of socio-economic activities which ultimately merged with the urbanised Harappan Civilization in the region. The trajectory of progress noticed at Mehrgarh continued to grow at a nearby site of

Nausharo, 6 km south of Mehrgarh, during the Mature Harappan period.

NORTHERN INDIA

The Neolithic Cultures in northern India, (Kashmir Valley) are represented by a large number of sites above the flood-plains of River Jhelum, but the most important among them are **Burzahom** (north-east of Srinagar) and **Gufkral** (south-east of Srinagar). These are multi-cultural sites which reveal, besides Neolithic phase, the evidence of Megalithic and early Historical periods. The cultural process in the valley is divided broadly into two phases to highlight the change and continuity in its subsistence economy, and these are assigned to a time bracket of 2500 BC – 2000 BC and 2000 BC – 1500 BC, respectively. At Gufkral, there is an evidence of aceramic phase, i.e., the phase before the introduction of pottery when man was still learning the food value of plants, and it goes back to 2800 BC [Possehl and Rissman: 1992: 480]. An important feature of the northern Neolithic is the absence of a preceding microlithic industry.

In the first phase, people lived in underground pits, circular or rectangular, with a wooden roof-cover overhead for protection from cold. It is indicated by the post-holes on the mouth of the pits. In the later period, the underground chambers were abandoned and overground dwelling units of mud or mud-bricks came into use. The life-pattern too showed greater advancement. The people domesticated sheep, goat, cattle and also dogs and pigs. They cultivated wheat, barley, lentils and common peas. As per Allchin's observation [1997: 105], the meat element in diet was "markedly reduced" in the final phase of the Neolithic period.

The Neolithic people used a variety of tools and weapons fashioned on stone and bone. The stone tools included polished axes, points, pestles, querns and also the 'harvesters.' The 'harvesters' are rectangular stone knives with two or more holes on the blunt side. D.P. Agrawal [2002: 179] points out that this type of tool is not found anywhere in India, but may be noticed in the Chinese Neolithic sites. The bone industry at Burzahom is most developed of all the Neolithic cultures of India and forms its distinctive feature. It comprises harpoons, needles, arrowheads, spear-joints, daggers, etc.

The pottery is generally handmade, but the wheel-turned pottery appears at a later stage and includes bowls, high-necked jars, etc. The mat impression on the pottery, particularly on its bottom, indicates the knowledge of weaving. About a thousand beads of carnelian and agate found in a wheel-made pot suggest a trade contact with the regions of Rajasthan and Gujarat, the source areas of these stones. Similarly, a painted pot with a horned figure of a "deity"(?) like the one found at Kot Diji (Sind) may indicate cultural contact between these two regions, but the process of contact is not clear. Reference may also be made to a stone slab containing an engraving depicting a hunting scene in which an antler deer is being attacked by two men with spear and bow and arrow from back and front. The slab also contains the figures of two suns and a dog. It is suggested that this engraving may have some ritualistic significance.

The burial practice in the Kashmir Valley furnishes some interesting data. The burials are found in the residential areas or house compounds. Both primary and secondary burials were practised — the former contained the whole skeleton while in the latter only a few bones were buried. Red ochre has been found sprinkled on the human bodies. However, the ritual significance of ochre, if any, cannot be correctly ascertained. An evidence of a human skull with holes has been taken to suggest the prevalence of the ancient surgical practice of trepanning or drilling to draw out excessive fluid. At times, animal bones, generally of dogs are found alongwith human bones. It indicates the practice of burying the pets along with their masters. Another interesting feature is the ritualistic burial of a group of animals. In one case five dogs are found buried with an antler. Other animals represented in the burials include deer, wolf, pig, humped cattle, sheep, goat, etc. The horse, however, is missing at all levels.

In short, the Kashmir Valley on account of its special features such as pit dwellings, the use of 'harvesters,' prolific use of bone tools fashioned out of antlers, the practice of placing the domestic dogs in the graves of their masters, the ritualistic sacrifice of animals, and the use of red ochre on the dead bodies occupies a distinctive place in the Neolithic Cultures of India. So far there has been no indication that the Neolithic Cultures of Kashmir had any direct contact with the Harappan Culture which was existing contemporaneously and as it appears, they developed and existed independently. The evidence of horned "figure" on a pot and the discovery of a large number of beads of non-locally available agate and carnelian may indicate some relationship with other contemporary cultures of the period, but the nature and process of this contact is not clear. It is suggested that as the tradition of pit-dwellings and the practice of burying dogs with their masters are noticed at the Chinese Neolithic sites, Kashmir Neolithic Cultures may have been closer to the Chinese rather than other Neolithic cultures in India. But here again the picture is not clear.

CENTRAL INDIA

In central India, the evidence of the Neolithic settlements has come from various sites in the Vindhayan region of Uttar Pradesh and Madhya Pradesh, i.e., the area bound by Ganges in the north and River Son in the south. Among the important sites, mention may be made of **Koldihwa** and **Mahagara** in the Belan Valley (Distt. Allahabad, UP), Sinduria in Mirzapur Distt., and Kunjun in the Sidhi Distt. of Madhya Pradesh. The chronology of these cultures is beset with difficulties. While Allchin [1997: 94] places them between 4000 BC – 2500 BC, Possehl and Rissman [1992: 474] assign them to a calibrated time range from 3500 BC – 1250 BC. However, there are others who believe that the beginning of Neolithic culture at Koldihwa may be pushed back to 6000 BC.

The Neolithic people lived in wattle-and-daub hutments. It is indicated by the presence of reed or split bamboo impressions on burnt clay. The post-holes on the periphery of the floor suggest a temporary roof over-head. Since these cultures developed out of the preceding Mesolithic phase, both microlithic and neolithic tools have been recovered. These include blades, flakes, lunates as well as polished and ground axes and celts. These were fashioned on different material such as chalcedony, agate, quartz and basalt. There are also heavy tools such as querns and pestles which are associated with crushing of grains. From Mahadah come some bone implements. This site has also reported a cattle pen. The ceramic used by the people was hand-made and poorly-fired. It is of coarse clay with straw and rice-husk used as tempering material. The principal ware is 'corded-ware' or cord-impressed ware of different types including bowls and storage jars. The wares sometimes contain incised designs in the form of criss-cross or zig-zag lines.

The sites of Koldihwa and Mahagara furnish ample evidence of farming and animal husbandry. The bones of cattle recovered from here include those of cattle, sheep, goat, deer etc. Bones of turtles and fish have also been recovered. The most important feature of this region, however, is the cultivation of rice. The evidence for it comes from the carbonised seeds as well as from the rice-husk embedded in the pottery. These rice remains are believed to be of cultivated variety. As Chopani-Mando, a nearby site of the late Mesolithic period dated to c. 6000 has reported a wild variety of rice, its cultivation and domestication during the Neolithic period at Koldihwa, it is argued, may not be treated as a matter of surprise.

The scholars, however, are sharply divided in their opinion on the date and dispersal of rice cultivation in India. The earliest evidence of it that comes from Koldihwa is dated by G.R. Sharma and others [1980] to around 5500 BC. It tends to bring India at par with China where the evidence of rice cultivation goes back to 6000 BC and suggests that India may be one of the earliest places where rice cultivation began. Other scholars [Allchin 1997: 97-8; Chakrabarti: 1999: 207] however express their reservations and feel that the early dates proposed for Koldihwa need to be re-examined. In the opinion of Possehl too [1999: 246], these dates are incorrect. He believes that the earliest evidence of the use of domesticated rice in the subcontinent comes from Pirak in north-west India from 1800 BC, and argues that rice cultivation in India may have begun in the Mature Harappan period during 2600 BC – 1900 BC. D.P. Agrawal [2002: 180] takes another extreme view and suggests that rice-cultivation in central India may go back to the early Holocene period, i.e., around 8000 BC. With regard to the dispersal of rice cultivation in India, many scholars, on the basis of some similarity in linguistic terms between the languages of South-East Asia and eastern India, believe that it might have travelled alongwith the migrants from South China to central India via South-East Asia and Brahmaputra Valley. But there are many other who feel that rice cultivation might have started in central India and other regions in the subcontinent independent of any outside influence, maybe on account of the wetter climate in the post-"Ice-age" period. The controversy, however, goes on.

In short, the Neolithic cultures of central India developed out of the preceding Mesolithic Cultures but were distinguished from them by certain important features which included polished tools, domestication of animals, presence of cattle pen, and, most importantly, the cultivation of rice.

MID-GANGETIC REGION

The important Neolithic sites reported from the mid-Gangetic region are Narhan (on the banks of the River Saryu), Imlidih (on a stream called Kuwana), and Sohgaura (on the River Rapti) near Gorakhpur in U.P.; and, Chirand (on the banks of River Ghaghra in Distt, Saran), Teradih (Bodhgaya), Senuwar (near Sasaram) in Bihar. Among these **Chirand** may be taken as a representative site. It has revealed cultural material belonging to the Neolithic, Chalcolithic and Iron Age phases. The beginning of Neolithic culture here is dated from 2100 BC to 1400 BC.

The people lived, as elsewhere, in circular or semi-circular huts, made of reed and bamboo, often plastered with mud (wattle and daub houses). It is evident from the impression of reed on the burnt pieces of clay. The post-holes to support a roof and hearths for cooking have also been noticed.

The Neolithic people of Chirand practised plant cultivation and animal domestication. The cereals known to them included rice, wheat, barley, moong, masur. The knowledge of these plant foods, according to V.D. Misra [1999: 247], suggests that the people were raising two crops a year (winter and autumn). It may, however, be noted that the growth of agriculture in the region did not have much impact on the economic life of the people as the yield was still limited on account of vast forests which could not be cleared with the primitive stone tools. The bones of ox, buffalo, elephant, rhino, etc. have been found, and of these the first two were certainly domesticated.

The stone tools found include microliths such as blades, lunates and arrowheads fashioned on chalcedony, agate or jasper, and also the neoliths such as polished axes, querns and pestles made of quartzite, basalt and granite.

The bone and antler objects constitute an important feature of the Neolithic culture of the mid-Gangetic valley, and Chirand as well as other sites in the region have reported plenty of such objects which include needles, scrapers, borers and arrowheads. The bone ornaments such as pendants, bangles and earrings have also been obtained. As a matter of fact, besides Burzahom in the Kashmir valley, Chirand is the only Neolithic site in India to produce bone objects in such large quantity and variety. Terracotta figurines of humped bulls and birds have also been reported. All these indicate a growth in craft activity.

The pottery of the period is generally coarse and handmade. There is, however, some evidence of wheel-turned pottery too. The principal pottery types include vase, jars, bowls, spoons or ladles. Decorations, though not very common, consist of post-firing painted designs in the form of criss-cross, wavy lines or concentric circles.

In short, the Neolithic cultures of the mid-Gangetic Valley coincide with the declining phase of the Harappan Civilization and were marked by the prolific use of bone objects and the cultivation of rice, besides other cereals.

EASTERN INDIA

The important sites which have yielded evidence of Neolithic cultures in the eastern zone include Barudih (Distt. Singhbhum) in Jharkhand; Kuchai (Distt. Mayurbhanj) and Golabai Sasan (Distt. Puri) in Orissa; Daojali Hading (in North Cachar Hills) and Sarutaru (Distt. Kamrup, 24 km north-east of Gauhati) in Assam. The earlier phase at Pandu Rajar Dhibi in the Ajay Valley of West Bengal has also reported Neolithic artifacts.

On account of limited explorations and excavations in the region, the data available to us is scanty and even the chronology is uncertain. But as it appears, the people used a variety of tools which included polished axes and adzes fashioned on basalt or quartzite. Shouldered axes have also been reported from various sites particularly in Assam. Since this type of axe is widely distributed in South-East Asia, it is considered by some scholars to be an import in to India from outside.

The people had started domestication of sheep, goat and cattle, though hunting continued to be their main occupation. No grain has been found, but the presence of querns and mullers along with hand-made pottery suggests some kind of agricultural activity among the people.

The majority of potsherds found in Assam belong to the hand-made vessels of coarse clay and carry cord impression. It suggests that the vessels were enlarged and shaped by beating with a wooden mallet (hammer) wrapped with a cord.

It is pointed out that as this cord-impressed pottery has close affinity with the pottery from China and South-East Asia, there may have been a close link between east Indian and South-East Asian Neolithic cultures and that the Neolithic cultures of north-east India may be dated between 2500 BC – 1500 BC [Agrawal: 2002: 201]. However, the process of this interaction and its chronology need further investigation.

SOUTHERN NEOLITHIC CULTURES

The Neolithic cultures in south India were spread over Karnataka, Andhra Pradesh and Tamil Nadu, and thus, geographically speaking, covered the area bound by the River Bhima (a tributary of Krishna) in the north and the River Kaveri in the south. The important sites pertaining to these cultures are Kupgal, Sangankallu, Hallur, Tekkalakota, Brahmagiri, Maski, T. Narsipur in Karnataka; Utnur, Palavoy, Kodekal, Budihal in Andhra Pradesh; and, Paiyampalli in Tamil Nadu. A combined testimony of dates from various sites suggests for these cultures a broad time-bracket from 2335 BC to 1350 BC (calibrated) [Agrawal: 2002: 219]. The ashmounds which are an accumulation of burnt cow-dung form an important feature of the south Indian Neolithic Cultures (see below). F.R. Allchin in 1960 suggested a west Asian origin of these cultures but today their growth and development is viewed in the context of earlier indigenous stone age traditions.

A syncretic view of the Neolithic Cultures of south India reveals that the people lived near the hills or hillocks. Their settlements were guided by the consideration of the availability of perennial water, plentiful games, pastures for cattle and raw material for tools. They lived in wattle and daub houses, and their hutments were normally circular in shape with a conical thatched roof. Hearths and storage jars have been found practically in all the huts. There are also small pits which were used for throwing refuge and rubbish.

The subsistence economy of the people was based on animal husbandry supplemented by farming. A variety of charred grains from various sites including Hallur (Distt. Dharwar, Karnataka) and Tekkalakota indicate the cultivation of millet, barley, horse gram legumes, black gram and green gram [Agrawal: 2002, 213]. Some scholars believe that the cultivation of millet and barley might have been introduced in south India from South Africa, but others doubt it and favour the possibility of indigenous growth of these crops. There is also evidence of domestication of animals such as cattle, sheep, goat, buffalo, dog, ass and pig. The bones of elephant, deer, nilgai along with those of fish indicate hunting and fishing activities. The occurrence of charred and split bones of animals in profuse quantity demonstrates that animal meat formed an important part of the diet.

The people used stone tools made of granite and sandstone, and these comprised ground axes, chisels, querns and mullers. The microliths such as blades, points and trapezes have also been reported. Though bone tools are rare in south Indian Neolithic cultures, some of these are reported from Palavoy in Andhra Pradesh. According to K. Paddayya, the evidence of working centres or workshops at certain places indicates that tools were made not only to meet the local needs but also for delivery to other regions which lacked suitable raw material.

The pottery used by the people in the early phase was all hand-made. The decoration was minimal and mainly consisted of incised diagonal or horizontal lines. The vessels were available in various shapes and forms such as jars, bowls and spouted pots. In the later phase, wheel-made pottery appears. It is argued that as spouted vessels and constricted necked jars of south Indian Neolithic Cultures are similar to those of the Jorwe culture of Maharashtra (1500 BC – 1000 BC), there may have been a close cultural contact between the two. The mat impressions on potsherds indicate mat weaving. The Neolithic period in south India was also marked by rock paintings and bruisings, the evidence of which comes from various places including Kupgal, also known as Peacock Hill, near Bellary in Karnataka. The motifs in paintings and bruisings include deer, sheep, goat, humans, etc.

The southern Neolithic people had developed an elaborate burial system and they practised extended as well as secondary burials, the latter containing limited bones. The dead were buried within the residential area, and in many cases within the house itself. The funerary goods consisted of pottery, stone tools, etc. Tekkalakota has yielded the maximum number of Neolithic burials.

Ashmounds

Ashmounds constitute a distinctive and to some extent, a controversial feature of the south Indian Neolithic Cultures. These are vast mounds of burnt cattle dung ash accumulated as a result of periodical burnings. There are well over a hundred such ashmounds concentrated around the River Krishna in the regions of Karnataka and Andhra Pradesh. The major ashmound sites are Kupgal (Distt. Bellary), Piklihal (Distt. Raichur) and Budihal (Distt. Gulbarga) in Karnataka; and Utnur, and Palavoy in Andhra Pradesh.

Several widely divergent views have been put forward about the origin and nature of these ashmounds. For example, while some consider them as deposits of volcanic ash of remote past, others date them to the medieval period and treat them as physical remains of women who performed sati after the wars between the Vijaynagar rulers and the Deccan Sultans. Another class of opinion links them with some sort of industrial activity such as iron or gold smelting. However, the absence of physical remains in terms of human bones or the traces of iron or gold smelting or brick-making in the ash rules out the possibility of any association of these mounds with the above mentioned views.

Robert B. Foote was the first person to recognize these mounds as a feature of Neolithic Culture, and his view was confirmed by the presence of Neolithic tools such as ground stone axes, querns and blades, in the ash. In his opinion, these mounds represented nothing special and were just formed by the repeated burning of the collected cow dung for cleaning the premises. F.R. Allchin [1963: 175 ff] endorsing Foote's view on the association of ashmounds with the Neolithic age, interpreted them as cattle pen areas and distinguished them from human settlements. Further, on the basis of ethno-archaeological data, he related the cow dung burning to some annual religious festival or function, such as ritual burnings during the Holi, Pongal or Govardhan Puja in India. He thus speculated that cow dung was deliberately burnt to secure some boon in the form of fertility or better means of subsistence.

Recently, K. Paddaya (2002: 80-111] on the basis of a detailed survey of an ashmound site of Budihal in north Karnataka, has put forward the view that the ashmounds were "regular pastoral settlements" situated in hilly areas having limited agriculture. Referring to Budihal, he points out that it was a big site which had separate areas for specific activities, such as cattle penning, cow dung disposal, human settlement, animal butchering, workshops to make and polish chert tools, etc. He further argues that some big sites like Budihal may have probably served as a local regional centre where periodic congregation similar to present day cattle-fairs were held. Anyway, the debate on exact nature and origin of the ashmounds, an important feature of the south Indian Neolithic Cultures is still on.

Conclusion

In short, the Neolithic Cultures are largely defined in terms of transition from hunting and food-gathering to herding and food producing subsistence economy with a sedentary way of life. It could become possible because of better tool-types and more conducive environment with the commencement of Holocene Age. The transition did not appear simultaneously in different regions nor was it uniform in all respects but still the Neolithic Cultures exhibited a considerable amount of commonality among them. For example, the Neolithic people used well-polished and ground axes and adzes called 'celts,' but the microlithic blade tools of the preceding Mesolithic phase also continued to be utilized. Bone tools were also used and they have been reported mainly from Burzahom (Kashmir Valley) and Chirand (Bihar), though also found occasionally from other sites such as Palavoy in south India. The domestication of animals and cultivation of cereals by the Neolithic folks is evident from the discovery of charred pieces of grain and animal bones. The presence of querns, mullers and storage jars also suggests the same. This period marks the beginning of the use of pottery which was largely handmade, coarse and ill-fired; aceramic stage of Neolithic is, however, reported from north-west and the Kashmir Valley. The dominant type of pottery used in the Vindhyan region, mid-Gangetic Valley and the north-east was cord-impressed ware. The evidence of wattle-and-daub hutments indicates a sedentary way of life. Pit-dwellings are the characteristic feature of the Kashmir Valley, though these are also reported from Sarai Khola in north-west India and Nagarjunakonda in Andhra Pradesh. Burials and burial-goods are reported from many sites, but the burial of pet animals is reported from the Kashmir Valley alone. The origin of Neolithic Cultures or the emergence of early farming communities in India is viewed today in the context of an evolution of preceding indigenous cultural traditions rather than as an inspiration or import from outside, whether South-East Asia or West Asia.

6

Non-Harappan Chalcolithic Cultures

Introduction

THE end of the Neolithic phase marks the end of the Stone Age and the beginning of the Protohistoric period — a period which is characterized by the use of Chalcolithic tools, the tools made of copper in addition to those of stone (lithic). It is a period that bridges the gulf between the Prehistoric and the Historic phases of Indian history. In Indian context, the Protohistoric period includes broadly three copper using cultures — the Harappan Culture, located chiefly along the river Indus and its tributaries; the Chalcolithic Cultures situated outside the Harappan zone, covering a vast area extending from western to eastern part of India and the Deccan; and, the Copper Hoard Cultures, so named as most of the finds have been recovered in hoards, primarily from the regions in western Uttar Pradesh.

While the Harappan Culture was urban in nature and was based on surplus agriculture, specialised crafts, inter-regional trade, fortified towns, art of writing, etc., the other two cultures were represented by farming communities and rural settlements with no pretensions to urbanity. These non-Harappan Chalcolithic Cultures were marked by limited use of copper implements (except at Ahar in Rajasthan) and abundance of stone tools. The economies of these cultures were more akin to non-metal using Neolithic people and are, therefore, sometimes termed as Neolithic-Chalcolithic Cultures.

It is argued that non-urban nature of these cultures was partly because of the geographical constraints. Whereas Malwa and Maharashtra in western India lay in the semi-arid region containing sticky black-soil, Uttar Pradesh and other regions in the east had monsoonal forests and *kankar* ridden soil. Both these regions could not be cultivated effectively with meagre and primitive copper implements which the Chalcolithic people possessed. These people were, therefore, forced to confine themselves to the narrow alluvial strips of the rivers. It naturally imposed a restraint on their ability to produce surplus or to create a situation for the growth of trade and towns.

These cultures are, however, significant as they represent the early farming communities in non-Harappan India. They serve as a base for the growth of surplus agriculture and urbanism later in the sixth century BC when, in eastern Uttar Pradesh and Bihar, iron tools became an important means of agricultural production.

Cultures Outside the Harappan Zone

Ever since the chance discovery of a Chalcolithic site at Jorwe (Distt. Ahmednagar, Maharashtra), a large number of sites belonging to Chalcolithic Cultures have been reported from the upper half of India from Gujarat to Assam and the Deccan **(see Figure 9)**. These cultures are named after their key-sites or the region to which they belonged and reveal broadly a basic uniformity in their settlement and subsistence patterns. The prominent non-Harappan Chalcolithic Cultures in western part of India are as follows :

NON-HARAPPAN CHALCOLITHIC CULTURES AND COPPER HOARD SITES

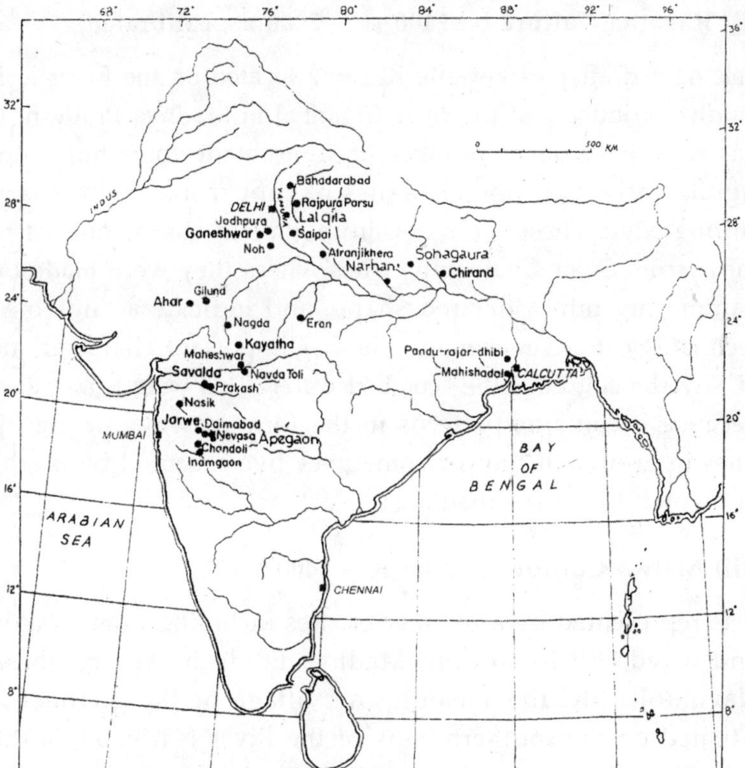

Fig. 9

(i) Banas Culture (*c.* 2600 BC – 1900 BC, calibrated)

It flourished in the valley of river Banas in south-east Rajasthan. As its key-site is Ahar, on the outskirt of Udaipur, it is also known as Ahar culture. Ahar, known as Tambavati (the city of copper) in ancient times, lies close to the Khetri copper mines and has yielded the largest number of copper artifacts in the form of axes, bangles and rings. Its nearby site Gilund has reported good amount of stone tools made on chalcedony.

(ii) Kayatha Culture (*c.* 2400 BC – 2000 BC, calibrated)

It is named after its key-site Kayatha located on the River Kali Sindh, a tributary of the river Chambal in Madhya Pradesh. It has reported a large number of stone blade tools but more significantly, two fine examples of copper axes with sharp cutting edge. These were cast in moulds in sharp contrast to those from other Chalcolithic sites where they were made by hammering into a desired shape, and indicate a "notable" technological advancement. Another important characteristic of Kayatha culture is the "combed ware." This ware is so called because it contains patterns in the form of wavy or zigzag lines in groups of four or sometimes five executed by means of a comb-like instrument.

(iii) Malwa Culture (*c.* 1700 BC – 1400 BC)

It is represented by a number of sites including Eran, Nagda and Navdatoli in western Madhya Pradesh. Among these Navdatoli, literally meaning a "village of the boatmen," situated on the southern bank of the River Narmada, is the most important and it has yielded the evidence of the cultivation of different types of crops.

(iv) Jorwe Culture (*c.* 1400 BC – 700 BC)

Its representative sites are Inamgaon, Sonegaon and Chandoli (Distt. Pune), Prakash (Distt. Dhulia) and Jorwe and Nevasa (Distt. Ahmednagar) — all in the state of Maharashtra. Inamgaon located on the terrace of a stream called Ghod, eighty km east of Pune, has yielded more information about the Chalcolithic way of life than any other site in India (see below).

Among **other Cultures**, reference may be made to Prabhas Culture on the Saurashtra Coast (c.1800 BC – 1200 BC), Rangpur Culture also known as Lustrous Red Ware Culture in the mainland of Saurashtra (1700 BC – 1200 BC), and Savalda Culture in the Tapti Valley, extending up to the River Godavari.

In northern and eastern part of India the important sites which have yielded the evidence of Chalcolithic Culture are Narhan and Sohgaura (both in district Gorakhpur), Imlidih (near Narhan), Kharadih (Distt. Balia) — in eastern Uttar Pradesh; Chirand (district Saran), Taradih (Bodhgaya), Senuwar (Distt. Rohtas) — in Bihar; Pandu Rajar Dhibi and Mangalkot (both in Distt. Burdwan), Mahisdal in the Ajay river valley of West Bengal and, Golbai Sasan (Distt. Puri) in Orissa. The site of Napchik in Manipur has also yielded some Chalcolithic material but its sequence is not clear.

As for the **Ecological setting**, the Chalcolithic Cultures flourished in two different regions which may be broadly described as eastern and western parts of India.

In the western region, the cultures of Ahar, Banas and Jorwe covered the area drained by the River Chambal on the one hand and the River Godavari on the other and included the Deccan as well. It was a semi-arid area and contained the moisture retaining black soil. It had access to different types of raw materials such as copper from Rajasthan, chalcedony from Malwa and Gujarat and basalt from Deccan for tools and artifacts. The crops grown in this area were largely wheat and barley though the evidence of rice has come from Inamgaon (Maharashtra) and Ahar (Rajasthan).

The Chalcolithic Cultures in the eastern part, on the other hand, flourished in eastern Uttar Pradesh, Bihar, Bengal and Orissa, and lay in the region marked by plenty of water and thick forests. These cultures were characterized by certain distinctive features. Firstly, for example, these cultures used larger number of the bone tools which have been found more profusely in comparison to those of stone or copper. It might have been because of the non-availability of suitable raw material for stone tools as also to the greater effectiveness of bone tools in the forest infested area. Copper ore for copper tools, which are otherwise scarce in number, might have been obtained from the Singhbhum area of Jharkhand rather than the Khetri mines in Rajasthan. Secondly, these were basically rice-based cultures, and it was probably because of the better availability of water in the region. Thirdly, these cultures in the eastern part of India, as the excavation reports reveal, evolved out of the preceding Neolithic Cultures in the region. Finally, the radiometric dates indicate that these cultures continued upto c. 700 BC, and ultimately merged with the iron-using urban cultures in the Gangetic valley. Thus, they fill the gap between the decline of the Harappan cities and the rise of "Second Urbanisation" in India.

It may, however, be noted that the non-Harappan Chalcolithic Cultures, though flourished in different regions and displayed some regional variations in their ceramic styles and cultural patterns, were marked by basic uniformity in various aspects. And it may be noticed in their mud structures, subsistence pattern based on farming and hunting and domestication of animals, use of wheel-made and well-baked pottery with decorative motifs in the form of wavy lines or other geometric designs. They also used a large number of microlithics (blades, lunates and triangles) as well as heavy tools (querns and mullers), latter as kitchen equipment. The evidence of copper tools is limited, except at Ahar in Rajasthan.

The **time range** of these cultures is mainly second millennium BC though, when calibrated, their dates, particularly at Ahar and Kayatha, have been pushed back by three or four hundred years, making them contemporary or part contemporary with the Harappan Culture. But what role did the Harappans play in the origin or growth of these Chalcolithic Cultures is not clear. In fact, the wide differences in the cultural traits of the urban Harappan and the rural Chalcolithic people had led scholars to argue that there was no direct contact between the two, but in the opinion of Chakrabarti [1999: 209], it cannot be completely ruled out. According to him, as the influence of the Harappans is known to have extended up to Alamgirpur in Uttar Pradesh and Lothal in Gujarat, it is quite possible that they could not avoid getting mixed up with the cultural flow of central India and the upper Deccan. The **authorship** of the Chalcolithic Cultures is also not clear. Sankalia, on the basis of similarities in pottery designs, once postulated the West Asian origin for them, but his view has not found favour with others. These cultures also cannot be associated with the early Aryans as they are known to have remained confined to Sapta-Sindhu region (Punjab-Haryana) only. Their possible association with the Later Harappans who moved towards the east after the decline and devastation of the Mature Harappan Culture is too without any definite evidence.

On account of lack of complete archaeological reports, our information on the general life and subsistence pattern of the Chalcolithic people remains hazy and it has led to a number of speculations and controversies. However, an analysis of the combined data from various sites such as Ahar (Rajasthan),

Navdatoli (Madhya Pradesh), Inamgaon (Maharashtra), Narhan (Eastern Uttar Pradesh) and Chirand (Bihar) does enable us to draw a broad picture of their settlement pattern, social and economic activities and religious beliefs and practices.

Settlement System

The Chalcolithic people lived normally in thatched huts with walls made of split bamboos plastered with mud. At Gilund (Rajasthan) and Nagda (Malwa), there is also some evidence of the use of mud-bricks. A number of circular huts have been reported from Navdatoli and other places. Some scholars believe that these circular structures may have been used for keeping fodder, but Dhavalikar argues that these were "definitely" meant for residential purpose. He goes further to add that a cluster of huts with a single hearth indicates a polygamous society. Basing his argument on the tradition of some local tribes, he points out that every time a person acquired a new wife, a new hut was built for her [Dhavalikar: 1997: 281].

At Inamgaon, huts were laid almost in a row with an open space in between, may be for a road or a by-lane. It may suggest some moderate form of town-planning on the part of the Chalcolithic people. Besides this, an important feature of the Jorwe settlement was that the houses of the craftsmen such as potters and bead-makers were located at the entrance of the habitational area, a practice still followed in the Maharashtra villages.

The houses of the Chalcolithic period contained hearths or *chulah* as well as pit silos or jars for storing grains. In Maharashtra, there is evidence of the presence of a cluster of huts with only one single hut containing a hearth (*chulah*) and the storage facility. It suggests that the families may have lived in different huts but used a common kitchen, indicating the prevalence of a joint family system.

On the basis of the evidence gathered from western India and the Deccan, Dhavalikar [1997: 273 ff.] and V.S. Shinde [2002: 171] believe that these regions were organised in a "chiefdom society." According to them the various characteristic features of a chiefdom society, such as site hierarchy, developed craft specialisation, trade with other communities, special houses and burials for the chief, etc.; can be noticed during the Chalcolithic period in the region. As for the settlement hierarchy, V.S. Shinde identifies sites of different categories termed as regional centres, agricultural settlements, hunting units, factory-sites, and camp-sites for exploiting the local resources [2002: 162]. The evidence of a group of small-sized sites clustered around a larger and more important site such as Inamgaon or Prakash or Navdatoli suggests a two-tier site hierarchy with main control in the hands of some chief living in the bigger site. At Inamgaon, a large structure with five rooms, in sharp contrast to single roomed houses of the common people, with a "granary" adjacent to it has been identified as the residence of a ruling chief. It is suggested that the chief collected taxes in form of grain which was stored in the granary [Dhavalikar: 1997: 277]. Besides this, a massive embankment, maybe to divert flood water, has been reported from Inamgaon. It is argued that it is indicative of some administrative authority, political or religious, which alone could muster collective public effort to build such an embankment and enforce rules for proper distribution of water.

Some evidence of social stratification or a ranked society can also be gathered from the burials, largely reported from the Deccan. As it appears, the normal practice was that the adults were buried in a pit with the body laid in a supine position (flat on the back) with feet below the ankle chopped off so that, as per the prevailing superstition, the dead may not become a ghost and walk out of the grave. But one of the graves found in the above mentioned multi-roomed structure contains a four-legged clay jar having a skeleton of an adult male, placed in sitting, cross-legged position with the feet intact. This special treatment is indicative of the fact that this person was different from the rest of the community and might have been holding some high rank, political or religious. There is also a burial nearby containing the skeletons of two children wearing necklaces of beads of copper, jasper and seashell indicating their superior status in comparison to others. Thus, the evidence of social stratification as revealed from the burials in Inamgaon suggests that in Jorwe society there were some persons or groups who claimed the authority to collect tributes from the rest. The burials, in the opinion of Dhavalikar [1997: 280], indicate that it was a male-dominated patriarchal society. It may be mentioned that a skeleton reported from Golbai Sassan (Orissa) also has legs below the ankles chopped off. Whether it is just a coincidence or indicative of some contact with the Jorwe culture of Maharashtra, it is not clear.

Subsistence Pattern

The Neolithic-Chalcolithic Cultures which represent the early farming communities in India subsisted on agriculture, hunting, and fishing. They reared cattle, sheep, goat and buffalo which they also slaughtered for food. In the semi-arid region, the Chalcolithic people, according to Dhavalikar [1985: 687], appear to have followed dry-farming, i.e., leaving a piece of land fallow or uncultivated for sometime for earth to regain its vitality. The embankment at Inamgaon as noted above indicates the use of artificial irrigation by the people. A large amount of charred seeds collected by flotation at Inamgaon reveal that the number of crops which were cultivated here included wheat, barley, rice, jowar besides horse-gram, black gram (*urad*), green gram (*moong*), lentils and field pea. Rice and jowar are also reported from Ahar while bajra occurs at Rangpur. Normally one crop a year was grown but the Jorwe people appear to have raised two crops a year — rabi and kharif. Apart from cereals, fish-hooks and fish bones indicate that fish also formed a part of the diet of the Chalcolithic people. In Uttar Pradesh and other parts of eastern India various sites such as Narhan and Chirand have yielded the evidence of the cultivation of rice, wheat, barley, *moong* and *masur*. The evidence of rice which is quite profuse in this region comes in the form of carbonised seeds and husks embedded in the pottery. At Mahisdal (West Bengal) a large quantity of charred seeds of rice were found scattered on the floor.

Tools and Technologies

The Chalcolithic people had made a considerable progress in the field of arts and crafts. They normally used Black-and-Red pottery with painted designs in the form of parallel or wavy lines, dashes and dots. It was wheel-made and well-baked. It has been found in various shapes and forms including bowls, storage jars, etc. This pottery is termed Black-and-Red because in its interior up to the rim it is black, and the remaining part of the external surface is red. This biochromic effect is believed to have been the result of keeping pot in inverted position in the kiln. A big kiln has been reported from Inamgaon. Kayatha, as mentioned earlier has yielded a distinctive type of pottery called "combed ware" bearing incised pattern probably drawn with a comb-like instrument.

The pottery used by the people of Rangpur culture is termed as Lustrous Red ware.

Metal technology also shows advancement and it is reflected in many copper objects such as axes, chisels, knives, beads, bangles, fish-hooks, etc., which have been reported from various sites **(see Figure 10)**. Two copper axes from Kayatha, which are made in mould rather than by hammering, are treated as the finest examples of casting. Some of the many hearths found at Ahar, according to Sankalia [1969: 216], may have been used for smelting. It is believed that Khetri mines in Rajasthan were the chief source of supply of copper to the Chalcolithic Cultures in western India and the Deccan, whereas in eastern part of India it was the copper belt of Singhbhum and Hazaribagh in Jharkhand which was exploited by the people [Chakrabarti : 1999: 264].

The evidence of gold ornaments, though extremely rare, comes from some sites of the Jorwe culture (Maharashtra). One specimen of ear ornament has been reported from the site of Prakash. It is possible that the source of this gold was either Hatti in Gulbarga or the Kolar mines. Technological progress is also seen in the process of making beads of different materials such as steatite, agate and carnelian.

Trade Contacts

The Chalcolithic Cultures do not appear to have existed in isolation. The evidence furnished by the presence of beads, copper tools and gold ornaments, which were made of non-local raw material, suggests that there was some sort of reciprocal exchange or trade among different communities. Internally, similarity in pottery forms and fabric may indicate that pots were an item of exchange between different sites within a particular cultural zone. As it has been mentioned above, certain large sites such as Ahar, Kayatha, Navdatoli and Inamgaon might have served as the focal points of collection and distribution of goods of both internal and external nature.

Religious Beliefs and Practices

The data at our disposal is too meagre to review the religious beliefs and practices of the Chalcolithic people, but some scholars such as Dhavalikar [1997: 145 ff, 205 ff], D.P. Agrawal [1999: 472], and Shinde [2002: 168] have attempted to analyse the material obtained from various sites in western India in this respect. They suggest that there was a prevalence of the worship of bull and also of mother goddess among the people. Their argument is based on the recovery of a large number of terracotta figurines of bull from Ahar, Gilund and Kayatha, and those of females with big breasts from Nevasa, Inamgaon and other places. The bull figurines are made of fine clay and have a delicate modelling as reflected in their long pointed horns and a prominent hump. A painting on a huge storage jar from Navdatoli has been taken to represent mother goddess worship. It depicts a female figure, a deity (?), flanked by a woman (worshipper?) on the one hand and a lizard or crocodile on the other, with what looks like a "shrine" indicated by three concentric arches on one side [Dhavalikar: 1997: 145]. Dhavalikar [2002: 261] and Shinde [2002: 168] also believe that the people followed the practice of "fire-worship." This argument is based on the so called "fire-pits" reported from Navdatoli which according to them might have been used for performing sacrifices or some related rituals. But, as already mentioned, our data is quite limited and therefore all the arguments on religious life of the Chalcolithic people remain highly speculative and controversial.

The Chalcolithic sites were deserted around 1000 BC though at certain places they continued to exist upto 700 BC. Their decline and desertion is normally attributed by Dhavalikar to change in climate which around 1000 BC became more arid. The chemical analysis of soil profile from Nevasa and the pollen analysis of lake deposits in Rajasthan indicate a decline in rain pattern and the beginning of dry period from about 1200 BC [Dhavalikar: 1985: 78-9]. As the local people found it difficult to meet the challenges of the new situation, those settled in western India and the Deccan tended to move out to other places. V.S. Shinde [2002: 178], on the other hand, argues that there is "strong possibility" that these people were forced to move out of their original habitats after Megalithic people equipped with iron implements started arriving at the scene, though he concedes that he has no definite evidence to confirm it.

However, it is worth noting that unlike the Chalcolithic sites in western and central India, those in the mid-Ganga plain were not deserted. In the opinion of R.S. Sharma [1996: 33], possibly the non-availability of iron and its technology to the people of central and western India ruled out any expansion of the old settlements after the exhaustion of the fertility of local soil, whereas the people in the mid-Ganga basin did not face this problem and, therefore, several Chalcolithic settlements in this region gradually grew into full-fledged Iron Age settlements.

Conclusion

In short, the Chalcolithic Cultures existing outside the Harappan zone were non-urban is nature but still they mark a great progress and improvement over the preceding Neolithic Cultures. And this is evident in the use of wheel-made and well-baked painted pottery, introduction of copper tools and the cultivation of larger number of crops in different ecozones. These Cultures prepared a ground for a take-off for "Second Urbanisation" later in the sixth century BC when iron came to be used on a larger scale for productive activities.

Copper-Hoard Cultures

The term Copper-Hoard Culture refers to a number of Copper implements discovered accidentaly, generally in hoards, while ploughing a field or making a road. The first Copper-Hoard was reported from Bithur in Kanpur in 1822 and since then many such hoards have come to light from different parts of the Indian subcontinent extending from Rajasthan in the west to Bengal and Orissa in the east, and from Haryana in the north to Karnataka in the south. Even in Pakistan, the site of Shalozan has revealed the presence of these hoards. As the artifacts discovered show great similarity in shape and form, all these hoards have been clubbed together under the term Copper-Hoard Culture. The largest number of Copper-Hoard sites numbering forty are in Uttar Pradesh, followed by nineteen in Bihar and eight in Madhya Pradesh. Gungeria in district Balaghat (Madhya Pradesh) is the biggest Copper-Hoard site containing 424 copper implements, besides 102 thick sheets of silver. As these Copper-Hoard sites are chance discoveries, there is considerable amount of difference of opinion among scholars with regard to their date, authorship and archaeological association.

The important **tools and implements** recovered from the Copper-Hoards include hatchet or *parasu*, celts, harpoons, antennae swords and anthropomorphic figures **(see Figure 10)**. The antennae sword is called so because on its hilt there is a bifurcation like that of an antenna of an insect, probably for fixing it to a wooden handle. Harpoon is like a mid-ribbed

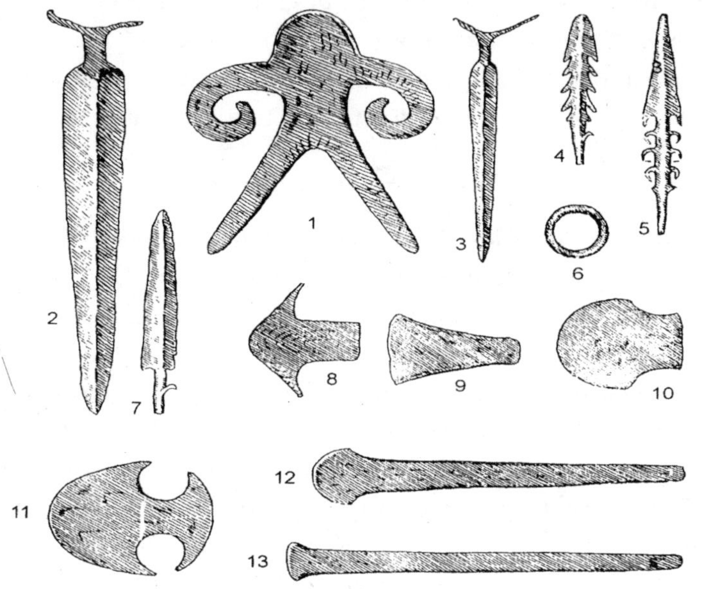

Copper Hoard Objects —
1. Anthropomorphic Figure; 2 & 3 Antennae Sword; 4 & 5 Harpoons; 6 Ring; 7. Hooked Spearhead; 8. Hatchet (*parsu*); 9. Celt; 10. Shouldered Celt; 11. Double Edged Axe; 12 & 13 Bar Celts

Fig. 10

sword having barbs, i.e., curved arms pointing backwards. It could be used for killing a fish or a big game as shown in a rock-painting from Mirzapur, Uttar Pradesh. The anthropomorphic figures are quite unique and have no parallel in the world. They are confined to Ganga valley alone. They are human shaped objects with incurved arms and spread out legs and curved top indicating a head. One such figure was reported from Lothal by S.R. Rao who associated it with the Harappan Culture. But, because of the uncertain date of the object, his view is doubted. Since anthropomorphic figures suggest human forms, they have been identified as some ritualistic or cult object of worship, though D.P. Agrawal argues that these could have been used as missiles or boomerangs to kill birds, etc. (Boomerang is made of a particular shape so that when properly thrown it returns back to the thrower. It is used as a weapon by the aborigines of Australia and other places). Interestingly, figures with similar shape, made in iron sheet, are still worshipped by certain people in northern India as the representation of Saturn (Shani).

An analysis of the copper tools recovered from the hoards indicates that they were primarily used in such activities as hunting, fishing and clearing the jungles. No agricultural implement has so far been found. In the opinion of D.P. Agrawal [1971: 98] the use-marks on the bar celts indicate that they were probably used for copper-mining. He also points out that the chemical analysis of the Copper-Hoard objects indicates that these were made of pure copper, having 98% purity and argues that the Copper-Hoard people might have received copper from the Chota Nagpur region of Jharkhand or even from Kumaon in Uttaranchal in contrast to the Khetri mines of Rajasthan which were a source of copper to the Harappan people [1999: 476-77]. As for the technology, the Copper-Hoard artifacts were made by hammering and cutting metal sheets as well as by closed casting, i.e., by pouring melted metal into a mould to harden.

Archaeologically speaking, it was B.B. Lal who in 1950s for the first time associated the Copper-Hoard cultures with the people using Ochre Coloured Pottery (OCP). His contention was based on the excavations at Bisauli (Distt. Badaun, U.P.) and Rajpur Parsu (Distt. Bijnore, Uttar Pradesh) where both Copper-Hoard tools and OCP were found together at the same level, suggesting their contemporaneity. It was further confirmed in 1970 when Saipai (Distt. Etawah, Uttar Pradesh) also reported the same situation.

The OCP is mostly reported from the alluvial plains of the Gangetic Doab and is called so because, as mentioned earlier, on rubbing it leaves an ochreous colour on the fingers. It is suggested that its ochre colour or surface was probably due to either its deposit for a long time in the water-logged area or ill-firing or both. In fact, B.B. Lal once argued that pottery called OCP might have been just Black on Red ware as used by the Chalcolithic Cultures of northern and western India. The OCP is found below the Painted Grey Ware (PGW) which is associated with the iron-using people. It is thus believed that the OCP related cultures did not have the knowledge of iron and represented a non-urban character of the society. The people lived in temporary huts or shelters and followed a mixed pastoral-cum-agricultural economy.

Though most of the scholars associate Copper-Hoard objects with the Ochre Coloured Pottery, M.C. Joshi and Krishna Deva [*Puratattava*: 1971-72: 13, 15] tend to strike a note of caution. According to Joshi, the Copper-Hoard tools indicate the use of highly refined and complicated copper technology, whereas the standard of economy reflected in the excavated material from the Chalcolithic sites appears to be very poor. In his opinion, these fine implements could not have been made by people of ordinary culture and might have belonged to the earlier Copper-Bronze Age, i.e., the Harappan Culture. K. Deva supporting Joshi's view also argues that the Copper-Hoard people who were so proficient in smelting copper could not have made such poor pottery as OCP. The real picture, however, continues to be dim and hazy.

Chronologically, the radiocarbon dates from Ganeswar-Jodhpura region in Rajasthan suggest that the OCP in that area may go back to 2800 BC, while the Copper-Hoard cultures of Uttar Pradesh appear to be much later in date and are placed broadly in the time bracket of 2000 BC – 1500 BC [V.D. Misra: 2002: 285]. These cultures are thus contemporary with the Late Harappan cultures which are dated around c. 1900 BC – 1400 BC, and therefore the Harappan impact on them may not be ruled out.

The question of **authorship** of the Copper-Hoard cultures is also not clear and has led to wide speculations among the scholars. While Heine-Gelden and Allchin, on the basis of some parallels and similarities between Copper-Hoard implements and those from West Asia attribute these hoards to Indo-Aryans while on their march towards India during 1200 BC, D.P. Agrawal [1971] on similar grounds of similarity finds South-East Asian inspiration behind these cultures. In the opinion of B.B. Lal these cultures could be pre-Aryan and he associates them with the Munda or other aboriginal tribes of northern India. R.C. Gaur suggests that these Copper-Hoards might have belonged to the early Vedic Aryans, while V.N. Misra and D.K. Chakrabarti link them with the Late Harappans.

Though the question of authorship is still being debated, some points in this context need to be noted. Firstly, the presence of similar type of tools in far flung areas, either in West Asia or South-East Asia, is not enough to suggest their interrelation unless the process of contact is made clear through intermediary sites. Secondly, it is doubtful whether Mundas or other local aborigines had enough technological skill to make such sophisticated implements as found in the Copper-Hoards. Thirdly, the Vedic Aryans too may not have been associated with the Copper-Hoards, because, as the Rigveda suggests, their area of influence was mainly confined to *Sapta*

Sindhu, i.e., the region west of River Yamuna whereas most of the Copper-Hoards have been located in the east of that river. In this scenario, there is only one possibility, i.e., the Copper-Hoards might have been associated with the Late Harappans who after the decline of the Harappan Culture in around 1900 BC moved eastwards and dispersed their knowledge of copper technology in the local areas. The presence of the Late Harappan Ware together with the OCP at Ambakheri and Bargaon, both in western Uttar Pradesh, indicates the possibility of association between the Late Harappans and the local people [Chakrabarti: 1999]. Though some tool-types such as antennae swords or harpoons have not been found in the Harappan assemblages, their association with the Late Harappans cannot be ruled out. As V.D. Misra [2002: 283] argues, the Harappan cultural zone was arid in nature whereas the Copper-Hoards in the Upper Ganga Valley lay in a different climatic zone having higher rainfall and dense forestation, and it is thus quite possible that the Late Harappans, after having left the Indus region, invented new types of tools to adjust themselves to new ecological situation. Anyway, there is as yet no final word on the Copper-Hoard Cultures and the debate on their origin, authorship and archaeological significance continues.

Appendix-I

Megalithic Cultures (Peninsular India and the Deccan c. 1000 BC – 300 BC)

Introduction

THE period from c. 1000 BC to 300 BC in south India and the Deccan was marked by the presence of Megalithic cultures. The term "megalithic" is derived from the Greek words *megas*, i.e., huge and *lithos*, i.e., stone. The Megaliths are thus structures built of large, undressed or roughly dressed, stones erected normally in the memory of the dead and occur generally above the ground. These monuments have been discovered from various regions of the Indian subcontinent and reveal a great variation in their forms and structures, yet they represent, in the Indian context, a homogeneous culture dominated by two key elements — a) use of iron tools and weapons and, b) familiarity with a polished and well-fired pottery called Black-and-Red Ware. The food-grains and artifacts found at the Megalithic sites indicate that the Megalithic people followed for their subsistence agro-pastoral and hunting activities. They also indulged in craft activities and were proficient in making objects of various metals which, besides iron, included gold, silver and copper/bronze. Though the origin, chronology and authorship of the Megalithic cultures is still being debated, their historical significance lies in the fact that they represent the earliest iron-using communities in south India. More significantly, they provide an important evidence of linkages between the southern Neolithic-Chalcolithic cultures on one hand and the Early Historical period, characterized by the Satavahana rule in the Deccan and the Sangam literary traditions in Tamil Nadu, on the other. It may be noted that in south India there has been no Copper-Bronze Age but only the Iron Age that emerged straight from the Neolithic stage. One reason for it may be the paucity of copper as against the iron sources which occur in Hyderabad and Kurnool districts of Andhra Pradesh, Bellary and Dharwar districts of Karnataka, and Salem and Tiruchirapalli district of Tamil Nadu.

Distribution of the Megalithic Monuments and their Structural Forms

Ever since 1823 when Babington published for the first time an account of the Megalithic tombs in the Malabar region of Kerala, a number of new sites with a variety of Megalithic structures have been reported from practically all over India except the Indo-Gangetic plains, the Rajasthan Desert and the parts of Gujarat (see **Figure 11**). These are, however, largely concentrated in the region of peninsular India and the Deccan i.e. south of River Narmada. Moorti [1994: 4-5] who has recorded about 2000 Megalithic sites from south India alone points out that maximum of these are located in Karnataka which has 665 sites, followed by Tamilnadu with 607 sites, Andhra Pradesh with 300 sites, Kerala with 270 sites and Maharashtra with 91 sites. Among the important Megalithic sites reference may be made to Adichanallur and Paiyampalli in Tamil Nadu; Porkalam in Kerala; Brahmagiri, Hallur, Maski, Sanganakallu, Tekalakota and Banahalli, close to the Kolar mines, in Karnataka; Nagarjunakonda and Yelleswaram in Andhra Pradesh; and Naikund, Mahurjhari, Junapani, Talakghat, Khapa (all around the town of Nagpur) in

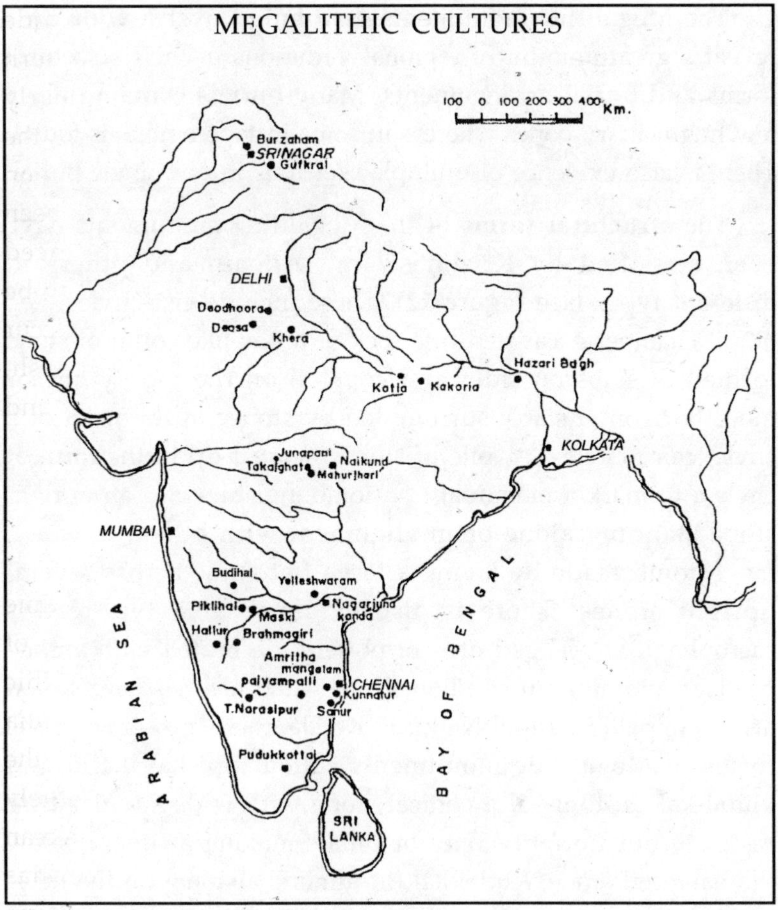

Principal Sites of Megalithic Cultures.

Fig. 11

Maharashtra. In northern India, these are found located in Allahabad-Mirzapur-Varanasi region of Uttar Pradesh, Almora in Uttranchal, Gufkral and Burzahom in Kashmir, and Leh in Ladakh. The Megalithic structures are also reported from the Baluchistan area in Pakistan. In north-east of India, i.e., Assam and Meghalaya, the Megaliths constitute a part of a tradition still living among the natives.

The Megalithic monuments distributed over a wide area reveal a great amount of regional variations in their structural forms and burial arrangements. Many burials contain only a few fragmentary bones whereas in some instances none is found. There is also evidence of multiple skeletons in one single burial.

The **structural forms** of the Megalithic monuments have been classified by Krishnaswami, Allchin and others in different types (see **Figure 12**). These include cist-circles, i.e., burial chamber excavated in a rock or a box-like coffin of stone formed of slabs on sides and covered on the top by one or more horizontal slabs, surrounded by stones in the form of a circle; cairn-circle, i.e., pile of stones heaped up in the form of circle a to mark a memorial or a tomb; menhirs, i.e., an upright stone standing alone or in alignment with others; dolmen, i.e., a tomb made by laying a large flat stone across several upright stones. There is also evidence of a type called sacrophagi, i.e., legged urns of pottery, decorated with animal heads, containing human bones. One such urn has been found at Paiyampalli in Tamil Nadu. In Kerala, there are some typical forms of Megalithic monuments called topi-kal/kallu and kudai-kal. In topi-kal a conical stone with wide circular base rests on four upright stones or pillars making a square below the balanced stone. Kudai-kal (lit. umbrella stone) on the other hand refers to a hood-stone which without any support rests directly on the ground to conceal the burial below it. In the Deccan, the most dominant form of Megalithic burial is the cairn-circle. In Kashmir, menhirs form a single form of megalithic monuments, whereas pits carved in rocks are more common in Mirzapur in Uttar Pradesh.

The Megalithic monuments similar in forms and shapes to those found in India have also been reported from other eastern and western parts of the world, but the inter-relationship between them, if any, is not clear. Some scholars

(Forms of Megalithic Structures)

Megalithictypes: 1. Menhir-2. Dolmenoid cist (or dolmen)-3. Topi-kal; 4. Kudai-kals (or hood-stone)- 5. Cairn-circle- 6. Multiple hood-stone- 7. Alignment (series of menhirs)

Fig. 12

such as Leshnik assign these similarities to the migration of people from foreign land to India, but many scholars today favour the idea of an indigenous origin of the Megalithic structures of south India. K.A.R. Kennedy on the basis of skeletal studies rules out the possibility of any large scale migration of people into south India from outside during this period. Parpola argues that the Indian Megaliths may have been Aryan in origin while Soundara Rajan attributes them to the local non-Aryan people. The debate on the origin of the Megaliths is still on.

Chronologically, no definite time period can be assigned to this culture. A number of C_{14} dates available from Megalithic sites broadly fall between the range of late second millennium BC and the early centuries of the Christian era. McIntosh [1985: 469], on the basis of combined analysis of radiocarbon dates and the tool-types, dates this culture from 1100 BC to 100 BC. U.S. Moorti [1994: 5] assigns it to a period from c. 1200 BC to 300 BC, and adds that the Megalithic traditions continued to linger on up to the early centuries of the Christian era. He prefers to divide the whole Megalithic period into two broad phases — early phase upto 500 BC, and later phase from 500 BC onwards, and argues that it was only after the sixth century BC that the use of iron, as in northern India, became more prominent in the economic activities, leading to agricultural and artisanal progress in southern India.

The **material culture** of the Megalithic people is reflected in their pottery types, metallic objects and the food-grains obtained from various sites in peninsular India and the Deccan which have been studied more deeply than those in northern India. One of the chief features of the Megalithic Cultures as noted above, is the use of Black-and-Red ware (BRW). It is made of fine paste and is wheel-turned and well-polished. It reflects advancement in ceramic technology, and includes such types of wares as bowls, lids and dishes. A significant aspect of the Megalithic pottery is the occurrence of graffiti marks on some of the pots. B.B. Lal once pointed out that these marks are very similar to the characters found on the Harappan seals and therefore, there could be a close relationship between the

Megalithic and the Harappan cultures. However, the process and the factors of this relationship are not clear. It has been argued that these could be just potter's marks.

Another distinctive element of the Megalithic culture of peninsular India is the plentiful use of tools and weapons made of iron. These include a wide range of artifacts for different purposes such as hoes, sickles and axes for agriculture; dishes and tripod-stands for domestic use; chisel and nails for artisanal activities; and, swords, daggers, spears and arrow-heads for war and hunting. The daggers had tangs (a long projecting point for a handle). Among other noteworthy finds reference may be made to head-ornaments of horses from Mahurjhari, near Nagpur in Deccan. These are made of copper sheets with iron-knobs.

The evidence of a furnace built of curved bricks from Naikund, near Nagpur, and of a large quantity of iron slag (i.e., rough waste left after smelting iron) from Paiyampalli in Tamilnadu suggests that iron smelting was a local activity in these areas. Moorti [1994: 42] refers to no less than 68 iron smelting sites in south India. The high percentage of pure iron found in the iron artifacts from Deccan indicates a great professional skill on the part of the local ironsmiths [S.B. Deo: 1985: 22].

The south Indian Megalithic people are the first to use iron in India and, therefore, their culture is sometimes described as the "Iron Culture of South India." The iron arrowheads and spearheads from Hallur (Distt. Dharwar, Karnataka) have been dated, on the basis of C_{14} dates, to around 1200 BC. It has led D.K. Chakrabarti [1991: 22] to argue that the earlier assumption that the beginning of iron in India should be associated either with the coming of the Aryans from north-west or with the supposed dispersal of Hittite monopoly of iron technology from West Asia should now be discarded.

He argues that, as iron artifacts found in southern and central India are of an earlier date than those recovered from north-western India, India may be accepted as a "separate" and "independent" centre of iron technology during ancient times.

Besides iron, the objects of gold, silver, copper/bronze, though found on a lesser scale, indicate that the Megalithic artisans were proficient in working out these metals as well. The items of gold such as bangles, rings, earrings and beads have been recovered from various sites including Adichanallur (Tamilnadu), Maski (Karnataka), Nagarjunikonda (Andhra Pradesh), Mahurjhari and Junapani (Maharashtra). Studs and beads of silver have been reported from Junapani and Nagarjunikonda [Thapar: 1994: 7]. The copper objects such as bangles and dishes have also been found from many sites. Copper lids of dishes with finials (tops) in the form of perching birds have been recovered from Khapa, near Nagpur and Adichanallur. The Megalithic people also used beads of semi-precious stones such as carnelian and agate as ornaments. Beads of shell and horn have been found at some sites.

A close analysis of their **settlement pattern** would show that the Megalithic people preferred to choose areas which could offer them necessary resources required by them. Thus, their settlements are found located near either a hilly area which could provide them stone for their graves, or the mining area from where they could obtain iron, gold or other metals for their tools, weapons and ornaments, or a water-fed region which could offer them an opportunity for agricultural activities [S.B. Deo: 1985: 94].

The structural remains at Brahmagiri, Paiyampalli, Hallur, etc., indicate small patches of floor with post-holes. It suggests that the Megalithic people lived in modest forms of houses made of timber. The size of the settlements varied from one hectare to eight hectares. It, according to U.S. Moorti [1994: 47], may indicate some sort of hierarchy of settlements. He has identified twenty-six large settlements which, as he believes, could have served as regional centres of political or economic power. The habitational sites of the Megalithic people discovered so far are, however, much less in number than their burial sites. The reason for it is not clear. Leshnik [1974] takes it to indicate pastoral or semi-settled agriculturist way of life of the Megalithic people but others believe that it could be because of lack of intensive regional survey.

The **subsistence economy** of Megalithic people was based on mixed agro-pastoral activities and their diet included agricultural products as well as hunted animals. The evidence, though limited, suggests that while people in central India produced items like wheat, barley and lentils those in farther south cultivated rice, millet, green gram, etc. In the opinion of S.B. Deo [1985: 90], the frequency of rice in southern sites may suggest that the Megalithic people in south India took more to rice eating than those in central India. He, however, argues that smaller floor area of the houses, limited quantity of food-grains and comparatively much smaller number of agricultural tools such as sickle and hoes in comparison to spears and arrowheads found at the Megalithic sites indicate that the Megalithic people were basically pastoral people with limited or marginal agricultural activity. But other scholars don't agree with him and point out that the available evidence suggests that the Megalithic society was composed of various social groups which, besides hunters and agriculturists, included specialised groups of artisans and craftsmen such as potters, ironsmiths, goldsmiths who could not have survived without some surplus production, howsoever marginal. The evidence of storage jars from certain sites also goes in support of this argument. It seems, as U.S. Moorti points out, the

Megalithic people in the beginning followed a pastoral way of life but later, particularly after 500 BC, when they started using iron on a larger scale, there was a gradual progress in the field of agricultural and artisanal activities, particularly in the riverine tracts.

In archaeology, the visible material remains of the past are treated as an index to the invisible socio-economic life of the Pre-historic societies. Thus, the objects found at the Megalithic sites throw light not only on the technological skills and craft activities of the Megalithic people, but also help us in gaining some insight into their social organization. For example, the presence of such items as gold ornaments, distinctive iron daggers with copper hilt, embellished lids of copper dishes, arrowheads and horse ornaments in the graves clearly imply that the person buried was not only economically important but also enjoyed special political or social status, may be as a chief or a warrior, in comparison to the persons in other graves with minimal of funeral objects. An analysis of grave goods has led U.S. Moorti to argue that the Megalithic people of south India had probably a "ranked society" dominated by a "chief." He is also of the view that the high percentage of adult males in the graves may in all probability indicate a patriarchal nature of the Megalithic society in which males occupied a special social status. However, in view of the lack of complete data, it is not possible to draw a full and final picture of the Megalithic society.

The question of economic or cultural contacts among contemporary Megalithic societies or between Megalithic and non-Megalithic societies also remains unclear. But the presence of non-local goods in certain graves does suggest some economic alliance or gift-exchange between different local chiefs. It is possible that the Megalithic people with their mastery over metallurgy might have entered into some sort of exchange relationship with the non-Megalithic people to procure the semi-precious stones or other goods in return for iron tools and weapons. It is noteworthy that many of the Megalithic sites are situated on the ancient highways or trade routes, and it is likely that some of these may have served as centres of regional trade or exchange. In this context, the presence of a large number of minor rock-edicts of Asoka (third century BC) in the region of south Indian Megaliths is quite significant as these may indicate an attempt on the part of the Mauryan king to collect and exploit the south Indian resources for the benefit of his empire.

The funerary goods placed systematically along with the dead bodies are indicative of people's faith in burial rituals and their belief in life after death. It is pointed out that ancestor worship is an important medium to claim and sustain the power of the succeeding chief and, therefore, it is possible that the megalithic graves represent the prevalence of ancestor worship among the people. But it is just a surmise.

Conclusion

In short, the Megalithic Cultures, though marked by diversity in time and space, are significant because of the use of a dual coloured (Black-and-Red) pottery and the development in the field of metal technology, particularly that of iron. The people followed for their subsistence a mixed agro-pastoral economy. The presence of specialised groups of artisans such as blacksmiths, goldsmiths, potters, etc., suggests that the Megalithic people did produce some agricultural surplus to meet the needs of their professional artisans. The significance of the Megalithic Cultures also lies in the fact that it forms a prelude to the subsequent economic growth in peninsular India and the Deccan during the early centuries of the Christian era.

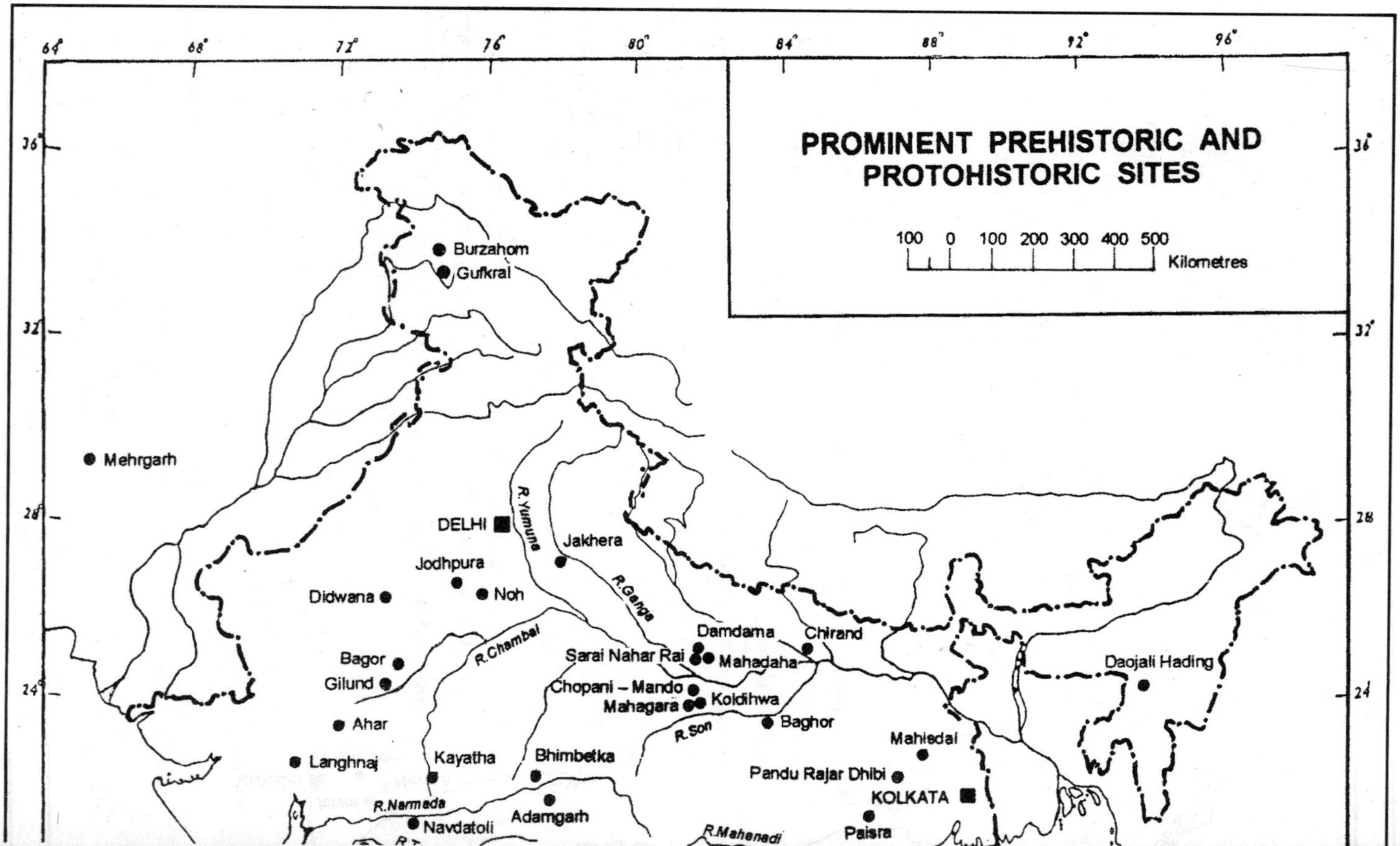
PROMINENT PREHISTORIC AND PROTOHISTORIC SITES
100 0 100 200 300 400 500
Kilometres
64°
68°
72°
76°
80°
84°
88°
92°
96°
36°
32°
28°
24°
Mehrgarh
Burzahom
Gufkral
DELHI
R. Yumuna
Jakhera
R.Ganga
Jodhpura
Noh
Didwana
R.Chambal
Bagor
Gilund
Ahar
Langhnaj
Kayatha
Bhimbetka
R.Narmada
Navdatoli
Adamgarh
Damdama
Sarai Nahar Rai
Mahadaha
Chopani – Mando
Mahagara
Koldihwa
R.Son
Baghor
Chirand
Mahisdal
Pandu Rajar Dhibi
KOLKATA
Paisra
R.Mahanadi
Daojali Hading

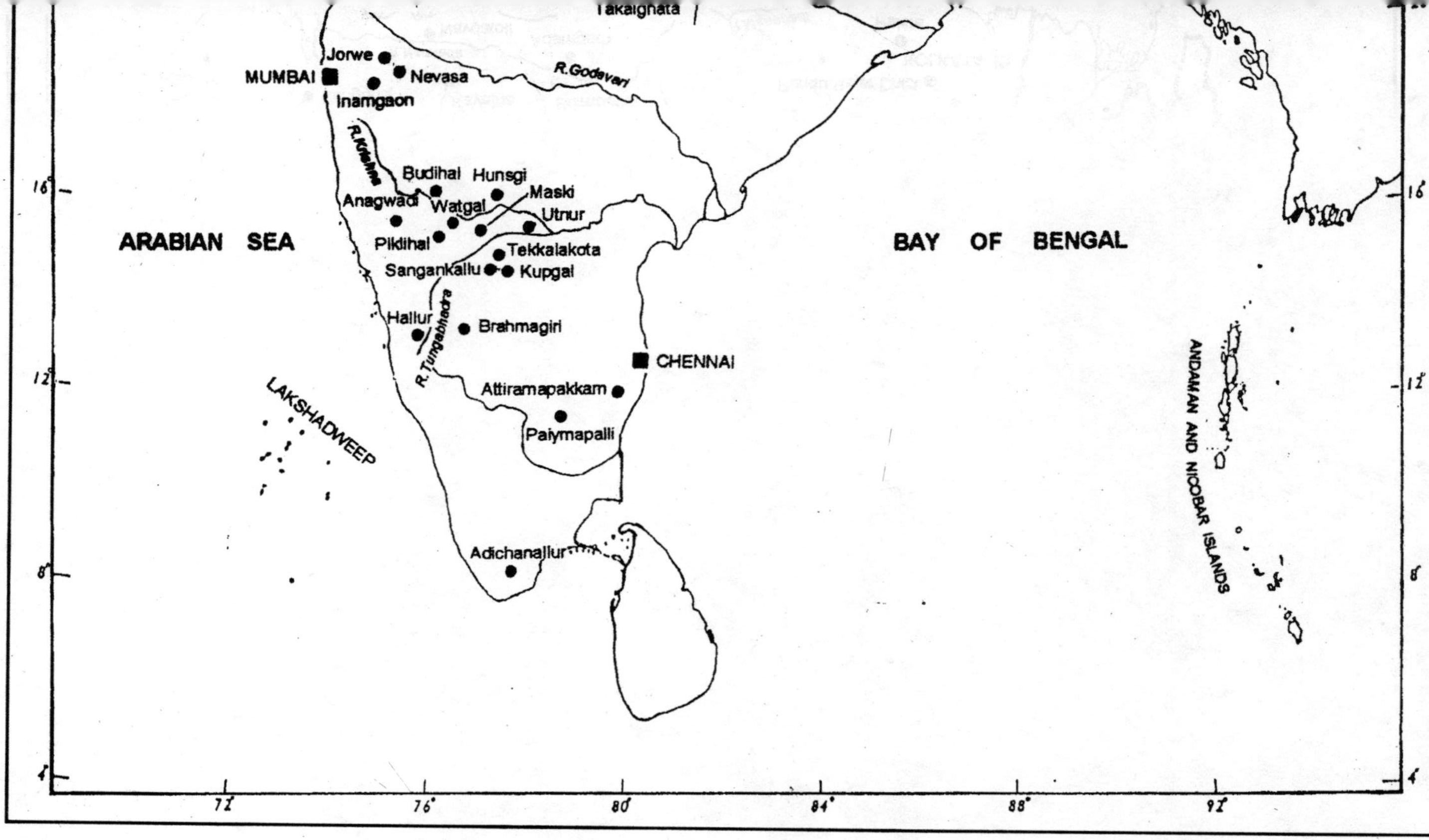
Takalghata
Jorwe
MUMBAI
Nevasa
Inamgaon
R.Godavari
R.Krishna
Budihal
Hunsgi
Maski
Anagwadi
Watgal
Utnur
Piklihal
Tekkalakota
Sangankallu
Kupgal
Hallur
Brahmagiri
R.Tungabhadra
CHENNAI
Attiramapakkam
Paiymapalli
Adichanallur
ARABIAN SEA
BAY OF BENGAL
LAKSHADWEEP
ANDAMAN AND NICOBAR ISLANDS
16°
12°
8°
4°
72°
76°
80°
84°
88°
92°

Appendix-II

Prominent Sites

Adamgarh

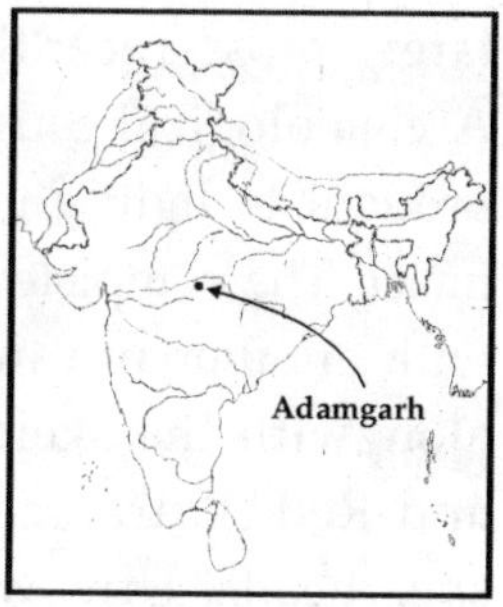

Adamgarh is a prehistoric site situated in the Vindhya hills, 2 km south of the River Narmada in Hoshangabad district of Madhya Pradesh. It has yielded Palaeolithic and Mesolithic tools as well as paintings in the rock shelters. The Early Palaeolithic implements are made of quartzite and consist of choppers, handaxes and cleavers, and belong to what is technically called Acheulian industry. The Palaeolithic phase is dated from 2,00,000 to 20,000 BP, whereas the microlithics of the Mesolithic period belong to the sixth and seventh millenium BC. The microliths in the form of blades, burins and also triangles and trapezes have been found in association with the bones of domesticated animals such as cattle, sheep and goat. As there is no evidence for the cultivation of cereals, it has been taken to indicate that domestication of animals in this area preceded the introduction of agricultural activity. Rock paintings in the rock shelters depict scenes of hunting, fishing and related activities and throw interesting sidelight on the subsistence pattern of the contemporary society. Wakankar who has made a detailed study of the styles and objects of paintings believes that while some of these paintings belong to the Mesolithic period, the rest are later in date.

Adichanallur

It is an urn burial site of the south Indian Megalithic Complex and is situated in Distt. Tirunelveli, Tamil Nadu. It was first excavated by Alexander Rea between 1885-1905 and later, most recently, in 2004 by the Archaeological Survey of India. It has brought to light a total of 157 urns out of which 57 are found intact. The complete body of a dead was put in the urn covered with another urn in a "twin-pot" system. The artifacts found alongwith the skeletons include pottery, particularly Black-and-Red Ware, copper bangles and earrings, and iron spearheads. Urns were inserted after cutting the rocks in the form of a pit, obviously with the help of iron implements. Adichanallur is believed to have been an important industrial centre. It is evident from the presence of a large number of iron tools and weapons which include axes, hoes, spades, and swords having different forms of blades. The remains of a potter's kiln and a smith's workshop have also come to light. The gold ornaments found in the graves include a diadem worn on the head. The evidence of gold diadem is intriguing as gold does not occur at Adichanallur nor at any nearby place, and must have been brought from outside as a result of exchange or trade contact. An important discovery reported in recent excavations is that of an urn having a graffiti or a short inscription in Tamil-Brahmi script dated to around 500 BC.

Ahar

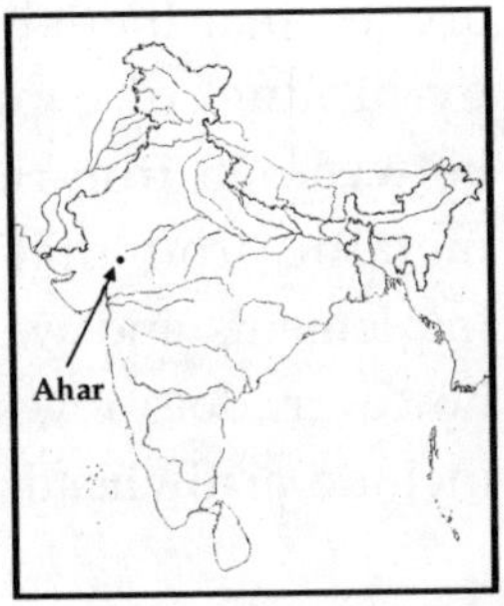

It is located in Rajasthan, about 3 km east of Udaipur on River Ahar, a tributary of the Banas. It is the chief site of the Chalcolithic Culture termed as Ahar or Banas culture. The excavations here have revealed two cultural phases, a) Chalcolithic, ranging from mid-third millennium to mid-second millennium BC, and b) Early Historical, belonging to the mid-first millennium BC. The later phase is marked by the introduction of iron and Northern Black Polished Ware.

In the Chalcolithic phase, people lived in thatched huts, rectangular in plan. There is evidence of *chulahs* for cooking. The pits were sunk into the floor to store grains. The main type of pottery used by the people was the characteristic Black-and-Red Ware decorated with paintings in white. It is wheel-made but coarse in fabric. A number of beads of terracotta as well as of semi-precious stones and shell have been found. But an important feature of the culture at Ahar is almost negligible presence of stone tools as against the profusion of copper objects such as rings and bangles. This might have been because of easy accessibility to Khetri copper mines. Ahar appears to have been an important copper smelting centre. It is suggested by the discovery of copper slags in a number of trenches. Some copper objects at Ahar reveal the presence of a high percentage of iron. It has led scholars to debate on the date regarding the beginning of the use of iron in northern India [Sahi: 1994; Chakrabarti: 1992; Tripathi: 2001, pp. 71, 72, 79]. While some on the basis of Ahar evidence argue that iron came to be used in India as early as around 1300 BC, others doubt the authenticity of the Ahar samples itself. In fact, it is argued that there is a possibility of iron being produced as a by-product of copper smelting but one has to distinguish between an iron-rich copper object and a definite object of metallic iron that appears much later for use as tools, implements and weapons. The early historical phase at Ahar, however, does reveal the presence of many iron objects which include arrowheads in large numbers.

Anagwadi

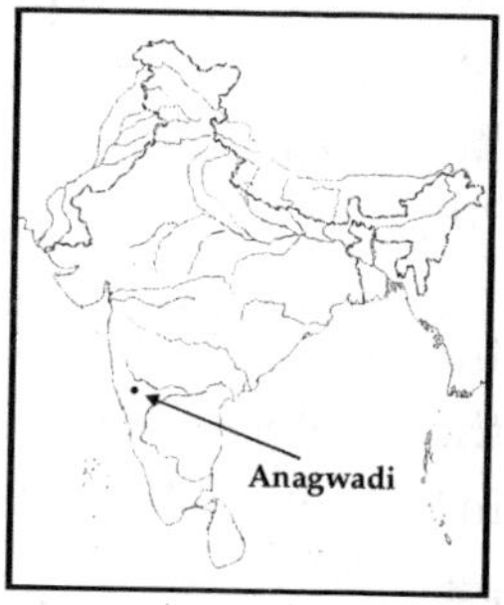

It is located in the Valley of River Ghatprabha, a tributary of the Krishna in Karnataka. The site is rich in both Lower Palaeolithic and Middle Palaeolithic tools which include choppers, scrapers as well as cleavers and handaxes of different varieties. Tools are fashioned on locally available quartzite, and there are indications to suggest that these were manufactured at the site itself.

Attirampakkam or Attiramabakkam

Situated in the district Chingleput of Tamilnadu, it is one of the key sites of the south Indian Palaeolithic (Madrasian) period. The work initiated by Robert Bruce Foote in this area in 1863 was followed by a series of excavations in the twentieth century, and these have revealed a gradual evolution of stone industry from the Lower Palaeolithic, i.e., Acheulian type of handaxes to the flake-based blades and points of the Levalloisan nature belonging to the Middle Palaeolithic period.

Baghor

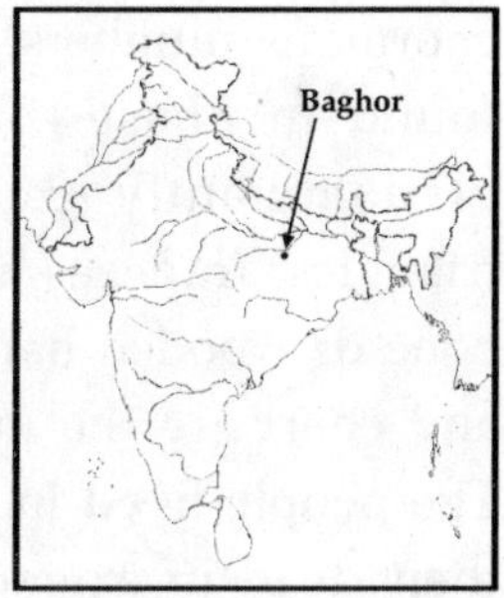

It is situated in the Son Valley (Sidhi district) of Madhya Pradesh. It has yielded a number of microlithic tools including triangles and trapezes made on chert and chalcedony dated to seventh-eighth millennium BC. An overwhelming predominance of waste material at the site indicates that tools were manufactured locally. The alignment of post-holes indicates that strong and sturdy posts were used to support the roof of the structures. The processing of plant or some other food is suggested by the presence of grinding stones. The hoof-marks noticed in the excavated area are identified with those of *sambhar*. An important structure discovered at the site is a circular rubble plate form with a piece of natural stone in the centre. It belongs to the Upper Palaeolithic phase and has been taken to represent, on ethnographical parallels, a symbol of female deity and the worship of Sakti among the local Prehistoric hunters and gatherers [Chakrabarti: 1999: 82, 101-2].

Bagor

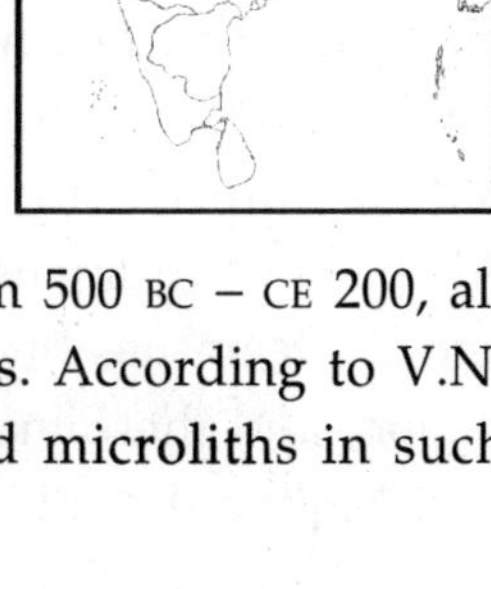

It is situated on the right bank of the River Kothari, a tributary of the Banas, about 25 km west of the district of Bhilwara in Rajasthan. It is the "largest" Mesolithic site excavated in India. It has yielded three cultural phases, Phase-I, dating from 5300 BC – 3800 BC, Phase-II, from 2500 BC – 1000 BC and Phase-III, from 500 BC – CE 200, all of which reveal the presence of microliths. According to V.N. Misra, no other site in India has yielded microliths in such enormous numbers as Bagor. The greatest density of these is found in Phase-I. The microliths at Bagor are truly and predominantly geometric in nature and include blades, triangles, trapezes and crescents which could be hafted on a bone or wooden handle to work as a 'composite tool.' Quartz and chert are the main raw materials used is making them. The people lived in huts with stone paved floors, and buried their dead in extending position in east-west (head in east) direction. There is no clear evidence of pottery in Phase-I but it is found in the subsequent phases. The only direct evidence for reconstruction of the subsistence pattern of the Mesolithic people is the animal bones found in large number. These include the bones of sheep, goat, humped cattle, etc. An area paved with small stones and containing a large number of animal bones has been identified as a butchering spot/floor. The fragments of querns and rubbing stones may suggest the use of plant food, possibly of wild variety. The economy of Bagor Mesolithic was, in short, based on a combination of hunting-gathering and stock-raising.

Belan Valley

It broadly covers the region from Allahabad to Varanasi in the mid-Gangetic Valley of Uttar Pradesh. It has revealed a complete and clear cultural sequence from Lower Palaeolithic to the Neolithic to the Chalcolithic periods. The Belan is a tributary of River Tons which empties into the Ganga, a little down stream of Allahabad. An intensive survey done in 1960s by G.R. Sharma and his team has brought to light many Prehistoric sites in the region, and these include Mesolithic sites like Chopani Mando and Mahadaha, and Neolithic sites such as Koldihwa and

Mahagara. There are some sites which have been categorized as factory sites. The data from the Belan Valley has been fully documented, and it is now possible to make out various stages of transition from hunting-gathering to the domestication of plants and animals. The recovery of rice in the burnt clay, dating back to 5500 BC, has led many archaeologists to argue that this crop may have been indigenous rather than an import from China or South-East Asia. However, some scholars are not prepared to accept such an early date for rice in India and doubt the authenticity of sample used for carbon-dating. An interesting find here is of a bone figurine belonging to the Upper Palaeolithic period. It, according to some scholars, represents a female deity.

Bhimbetka

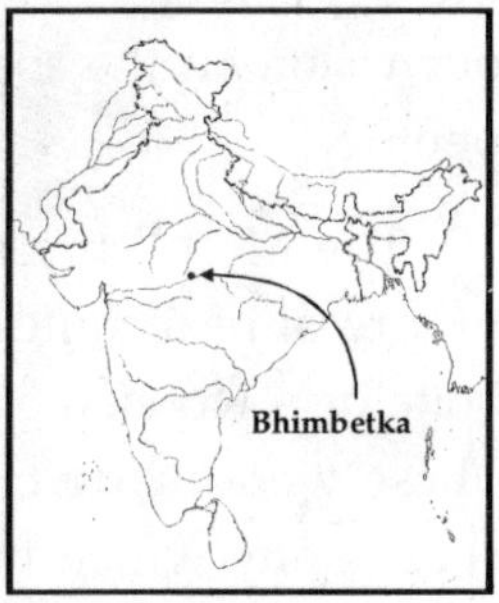

It is situated 45 km south of Bhopal in Raisen district of Madhya Pradesh. It contains a number of caves and rock shelters, formed by a natural process of weathering of the sand stone of the Vindhya hills. It has revealed a cultural sequence spanning the period from the Lower Palaeolithic to the Late Mesolithic. It has also yielded a large number of rock paintings belonging to different cultural phases.

Bhimbetka lies in the forest area having a variety of flowers and fruit-bearing trees and has a rich wild life and several perennial springs. It, in other words, has ample provision for the basic requirements — food, shelter and water — which must have attracted early humans to this area. Though discovered earlier, systematic excavations at the site took place in 1970s.

Of all the cultural phases, the Acheulian or the Lower Palaeolithic deposit is the thickest and includes tools like scrapers, cleavers and handaxes. In the following Middle Palaeolithic and Upper Palaeolithic periods, cleavers and handaxes disappear and flake and blade tools increase in frequency.

Mesolithic Culture at Bhimbetka is well-defined. An evidence of human occupation at many more caves in and around Bhimbetka during the Mesolithic period suggests an increase in population. Whether it was due to better climatic conditions with the commencement of Holocene Age or to improved tools and technology one cannot be sure. The animal bones and human burials belonging to the period as well as the depictions in rock-paintings greatly help us in enlarging our vision on the socio-economic activities of the contemporary people.

The Mesolithic people introduced microlithic tools made by pressure technique. These tiny tools could be hafted on a bone or a wooden handle to serve as knives, spears or arrows. These were made on fine-grained material such as chert and chalcedony which must have been brought from their source areas at some distance.

The presence of ash, charcoal, and charred bones of animals like cattle, deer and antelope attest the use of fire. The people buried their dead within the cave in the habitational area. By the end of the Mesolithic phase the regular occupation in the caves disappears, though some human activity continued with intervals all through the later periods. Apart from caves and rock shelters, there appear to be many open-air camp sites in and around Bhimbetka. It is attested by the presence of a large number of Acheulian and microlithic tools found scattered in the open.

Bhimbetka is quite rich in rock paintings. As a matter of fact, it is better known for them and has earned for this reason a status of World Heritage site. There are nearly six hundred shelters which contain paintings on walls and ceilings. These paintings have been assigned on the basis of thematic descriptions into three cultural or chronological phases — prehistoric, transitional and historic. The Prehistoric paintings primarily belong to the Mesolithic phase and are dominated by hunting and dancing scenes. The animals such as rhino, boar and elephant are depicted in different forms of activity, viz., standing, moving or running. Human figures are shown in a stick-like form, engaged in hunting with the help of spears, bows and arrows or collecting vegetable food. Women are also shown, sometimes in pregnant condition. An analysis of the Prehistoric paintings indicates that these belong to the hunting-gathering communities, and there is nothing to suggest that the painters had any knowledge of agriculture or animal domestication. There are also paintings depicting agricultural activities and warriors on horses but these belong to later phases.

Brahmagiri

It is situated in the Chitradurga district of Karnataka, south India, where a set of Asokan minor rock edicts (third century BC) were discovered. Excavated by Wheeler in 1947, it has revealed a sequence of three cultural periods : Period I, Neolithic Chalcolithic, dating to the early first millennium to second century BC; Pd. II, the Megalithic culture, from 2nd century BC to the first century CE; Pd. III, Andhra-Satavahana, from the middle of the first century CE to the third century CE.

In Neolithic-Chalcolithic period, the people lived in houses of perishable nature supported by wooden posts. An important feature of this period is the abundance of polished stone axes of dolerite. Microliths such as lunates, crescents and blades made on agate and carnelian have also been found in large numbers. Though some copper implements have been reported, the use of this metal is extremely rare. Pottery vessels are mostly handmade and have coarse fabric. The practice of putting the dead body of an infant in an urn (urn burial) has also come to notice.

The succeeding Megalithic period is characterized by the use of iron implements and weapons such as sickle, knife, sword, spear and arrowheads. The pottery is well polished Black-and-Red Ware. Graffiti are frequently noticed on the pottery. Rouletted ware is also reported in the debris. Among ornaments shell-bangles and beads of shell, terracotta and jasper have been found. An important feature of the Megalithic Culture is the disposal of the dead in stone cist i.e., an excavated pit enclosed by a circle of stones, containing funeral goods in the form of iron implements, beads, etc.

In the last phase (Andhra-Satavahana period), there is evidence of the use of better pottery made on fast wheel. Beads of shell, agate, carnelian as well as bangles of bone, gold, clay have been found in considerable numbers. There is also some evidence of brick structures. The whole archaeological evidence from Brahmagiri has been placed, as noted above, between early first millennium BC and the third century CE, but calibrated C_{14} determinations may suggest earlier dates for the Neolithic and Megalithic cultures.

Budihal

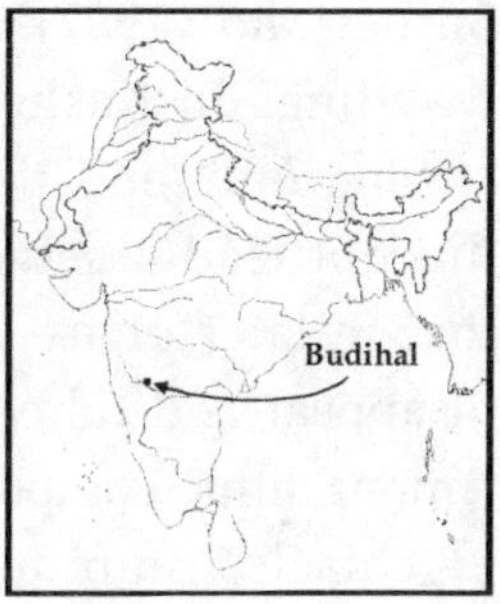

It is an important ashmound site situated in Gulbarga district of Karnataka. K. Paddayya, who has made a detailed study of the site, identifies within it distinct areas meant for different activities such as butchering, tool manufacturing, cattle penning, etc. The butchering spot has been identified by a scatter of smashed and butchered bones of cattle along with chopping tools. An analysis of the data from Budihal has led Paddayya to argue that ashmound sites have been habitational sites of pastoral people rather than just cattle camps as earlier suggested by Wheeler.

Burzahom

It is situated on an ancient lake-bed, locally known as *karewa*, about 2 km from the Dal Lake and 16 km north-east of Srinagar in Kashmir. It is primarily a Neolithic site but has also revealed the evidence of menhirs associated with the Megalithic Cultures. Burzahom, excavated in 1960s, is better known for its unique pit-dwellings, a developed bone tool industry and human-cum-animal burials. The earliest cultural phase at the site is dated to 2800 BC (calibrated).

The people lived in pits cut into the natural soil. These pits are circular or oval in plan, narrow at the top and wide at the base. Some of the deeper ones are provided with steps. Post-holes on their periphery suggest a thatched roof as a protective cover against the bad weather. Cunningham and

Sutherland [1997] who recently reviewed the so-called pit dwellings in Kashmir argue that these pits were meant for storing only and that the early Neolithic people of Kashmir did not lead a settled or sedentary life. Any way, it is true that in later phase of the Neolithic period, the pit-dwellings disappear and timber structures were raised on regular floors. Among lithic components at Burzahom mention may be made of chisels, pounders, mace-heads, and most importantly "harvesters" which are rectangular in shape with a crude cutting edge and two or more holes on either side. Bone tools are most prolific and form a diagnostic trait of Burzahom Neolithic Culture. These comprise harpoons for fishing; needles, daggers and arrowheads for hunting; and scrapers for treating hides. There is no direct evidence of the cereals grown, but a stone quern found in a pit does indicate the use of food grain in their diet. The remains of animal bones of cattle, sheep and goat, along with the presence of fishhooks indicate that hunting and fishing were an important source of subsistence.

Burzahom has reported numerous human and animal burials. Humans were mostly buried in pits dug into the house floors. A hole in the skull of a skeleton suggests the ancient practice of trepanning, may be to draw out an excessive fluid. An interesting feature of human burials is that sometimes pet animals such as dogs are found buried along with the dead in the same pit. Some burials reveal animals placed in a planned manner. It may have an association with some ritual practice. The animals represented in the burials are antler deer, humped cattle, wolf, goat, sheep, etc. The horse is missing completely. Among other important finds at Burzahom, reference may be made to about two thousand carnelian and agate beads found in a pot. There has also been found a stone slab with an engraving depicting a hunting scene in which an antler deer is being pierced from behind with a long spear by a hunter while an arrow is being shot by another hunter from the front.

In short, the important features which single out Burzahom, the chief site of Kashmir Neolithic, from the other Neolithic sites of India are pit-dwellings, stone harvesters, prolific use of bone tools, and the practice of placing pet dogs in the grave of their masters.

Chirand

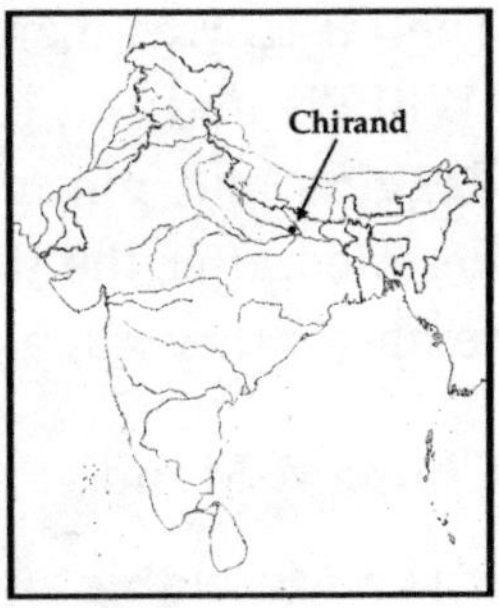

It is situated on the banks of River Ghaghra, a tributary of the Ganga, eleven km east of Chapra in Bihar. Geographically, it lies in the plains having alluvial soil and monsoonal climate. The excavations conducted here during 1960s and 1970s have revealed broadly five cultural periods extending from Neolithic and Chalcolithic to the Early Medieval period.

Pd I, Neolithic, dated to 2000 BC, was represented by stone hammers, querns, arrowheads as well as the beads of chalcedony, agate and jasper. The most outstanding feature of the Neolithic tool assemblage is the presence of highly sophisticated bone tools. These comprise hammer, scraper, chisel, needles, arrowheads, etc. There are also bone ornaments such as pendants and earrings. The bone artifacts are made either from antler or from long bones of cattle or deer.

The people lived in circular huts made of reeds and mud. There is also evidence of the use of hearths and Black-and-Red pottery. The discovery of *rice, wheat, barley, mung, masur* in charred conditions and also of a few burnt clay pieces with paddy husk impression bear witness to the cultivation of these cereals and legumes in the Neolithic period. Food of the people was supplemented by meat obtained from hunting and fishing. The above features may indicate that there was larger dependence on agriculture with hunting and gathering now assuming a subsidiary role and that both *kharif* and *rabi* crops were raised by the people at Chirand.

The following Chalcolithic period notices better and larger dwelling structures and is associated with the use of copper. The Pd III was marked by the Northern Black Polished Ware (WBPW) and the use of iron implements like axes, sickles, daggers and ploughshares. The site appears to have been deserted after the third century BC and was reoccupied in the tenth century AD, as the antiquities discovered reveal.

Chopani-Mando

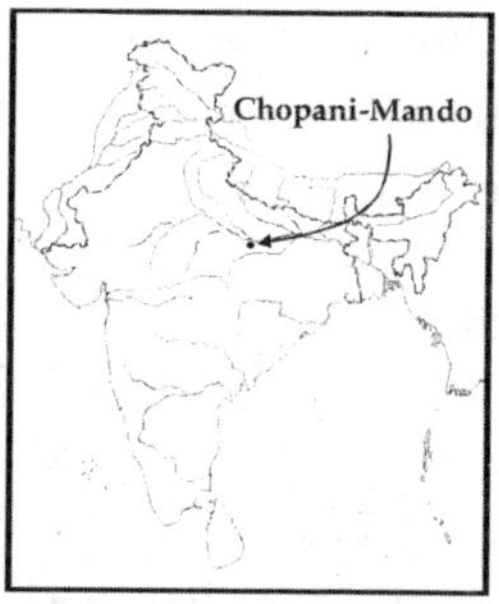

It is a Mesolithic site situated about 77 km south-east of Allahabad in the Belan valley in U.P. The excavations conducted here by G.R. Sharma in 1960s and 1970s reveal a picture of gradual transition in tool-types from Upper Palaeolithic to the Mesolithic period. In the earliest phase, the tools included blade, burins and borers but gradually they became smaller in size and geometric in form, and came to comprise lunates, triangles, etc., made on fine grained stones such as chalcedony, agate and carnelian. There is also evidence of querns, mullers and ring-stones along with huts having hearths. Some fragile hand-made pottery is also noticed. A few burnt clay lumps contain rice and rice-husk impressions. The excavators date the site to the seventh millennium BC, but such an early date is not agreed to by others. Anyway, the evidence from Chopani-Mando does suggest a transition from hunting-gathering to a settled mode of life, along with "incipient agriculture" during its latest phase.

Damdama

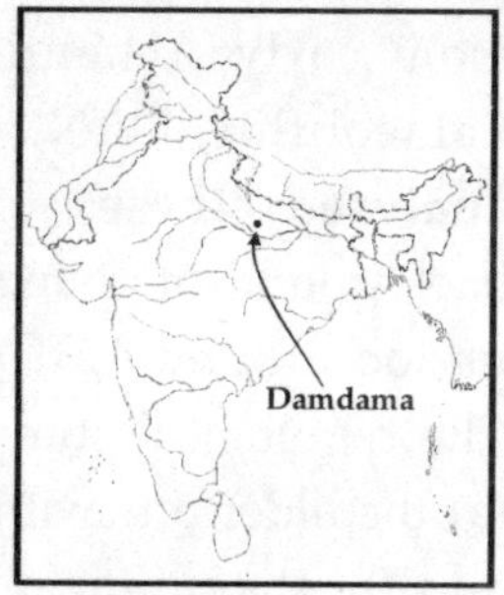

It is a Mesolithic site in the Gangetic valley, situated on the confluence of two branches of a small stream, Sai River. The occupational deposits have revealed both plain and plastered hearths, plastered floors, a number of microliths and bone tools, querns, besides charred wild grains and animal bones. Among the graves found here, there are two which contain two bodies each - a male and a female [Chakrabarti : 1999: 108].

Daojali Hading

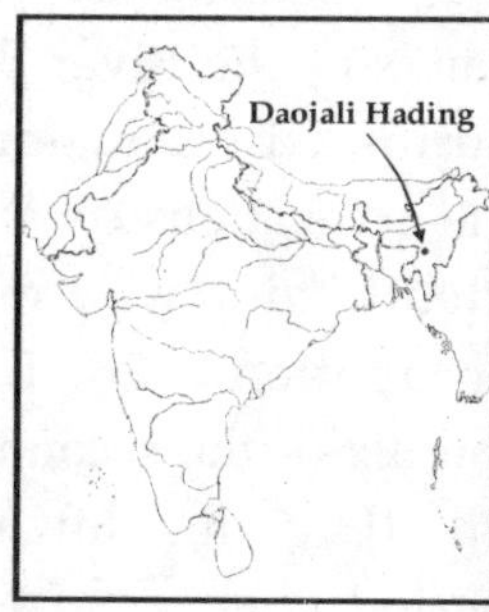

It is a Neolithic site situated in the north Cachar hills of Assam. Explored and excavated in 1960s, it has yielded a rich haul of polished stone tools along with potsherds but no metal objects. The implements found are classified as cutting tools and grinding stones, and include axes, hoes, chisels, querns and mullers. The raw material used for artifacts is a type of fine grained sandstone. It is suggested that presence of grinding stones along with a large number chips at the site indicates that tools were manufactured locally. The potsherds recovered indicate that pottery was coarse and ill-fired. Though no C_{14} dates are available, the site of Daojali Hading marks the spread of Neolithic traditions as far as north-east India.

Didwana

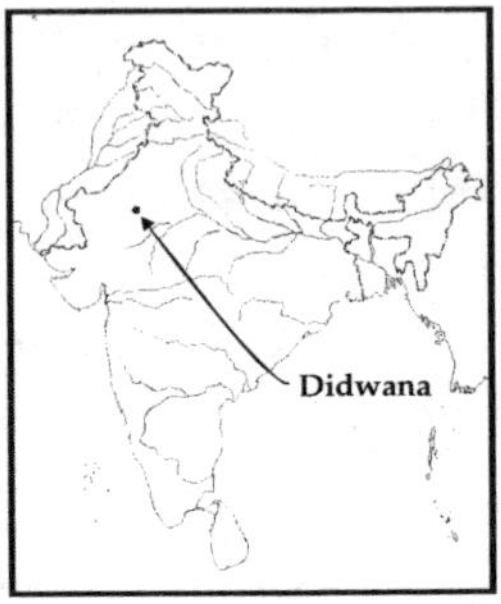

It is situated in the sand dune area of district Nagaur in Rajasthan. The excavations here have revealed a continuous evolution of lithic tradition from early Acheulian to the Middle Palaeolithic. V.N. Misra who has analysed these tools against the background of changing palaeoclimatic conditions suggests a period around 1,50,000 BP for the Middle Palaeolithic phase. The typological study of tools indicates two sequential stages, (a) the older one with the combination of core tools and bifaces, and (b) the younger one with small bifaces and a dominance of flake and flake-based tools.

Gilund

It is a Chalcolithic site situated near the banks of the River Banas, about 70 km north-east of Udaipur in Rajasthan. In the excavations conducted here, B.B. Lal identified two major periods of occupation - Pd. I, belonging to the middle of the second millenium BC, and Pd. II, going down to the historical period.

Pd. I, which is chalcolithic in nature has revealed the presence of microliths along with copper objects. The residential houses were made of mud-bricks, and within the house are noticed *chullahs* or hearths and also circular or oblong pits which must have been used for some kind of storage. The characteristic pottery of this period is a Black-and-Red Ware, painted over with linear or geometric designs in white.

Among the important finds at Gilund, reference may be made to the terracotta figurines of bull with a prominent hump and long horns. These are made of extremely fine clay and are well-baked. Whether these bull figurines carry some religious significance, one cannot say anything definitely.

Gufkral

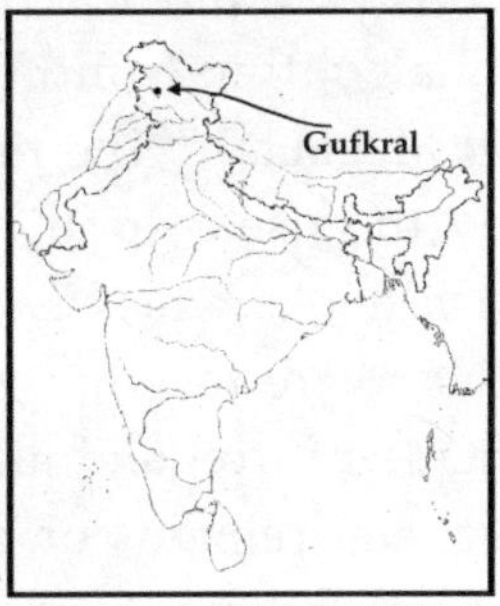

It is located in the Jhelum Valley of Kashmir about 41 km south-east of Srinagar. It was excavated in early 1980s. It is predominantly a Neolithic site, though there is an evidence of Megalithic Culture too. In the Neolithic period, people lived in pits dug into the ground. These were generally circular or rectangular in plan and were provided with thatched roofs as indicated by the discovery of post-holes around the edges of the pits. However, later, pit-dwellings disappear. Red ochre was used for painting the plastered floors. Along with polished stone tools, people used tools manufactured from antlers and bones. The latter included harpoons, scrapers and needles. The people domesticated sheep and goat and cultivated wheat, barley and lentil. The earliest phase of the Neolithic period reveals no evidence of the use of ceramic, and is thus called "aceramic Neolithic." However, later on first handmade and then wheel-made pottery appears on the scene. The impression of mat on the exterior of the disc-base of these vessels indirectly represents the use and manufacture of mats. The beginning of aceramic Neolithic at Gufkral may be dated to 3000 BC [Chakrabarti : 1999: 213]. The Megalithic level at Gufkral was characterised by the presence of menhirs and the discovery of copper and iron objects which are dated to around 1300 BC [Tripathi : 2001: 295].

Hallur

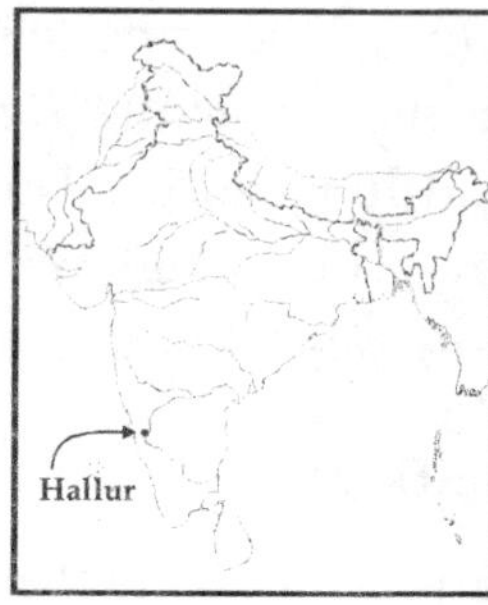

It is situated on the left bank of the river Tungabadra in Dharwar district of Karnataka. The site excavated by Nagaraja Rao in 1960s represents two cultural phases — a) Neolithic-Chalcolithic (southern Neolithic), and b) Megalithic. The first phase is marked by the use of polished stone axes, stone blades and copper fish-hooks whereas the Megalithic burials contain Black-and-Red Ware together with arrowheads, spearheads, knife-blades made of iron and also beads of bone, carnelian and gold. The vegetal remains of millet and the animal bones of cattle and sheep indicate a pastoral form of economy for the Megalithic people. A noteworthy feature of Hallur antiquities is the C_{14} dating of 1100 BC (1300 BC when calibrated) for the iron objects found here. It is taken as an indication of an early use of iron in south India. Korisettar [2002, 186] argues that early growth of iron industry in the south could be possible because of the fact that it has many iron sources whereas the supply of copper is greatly restricted.

Hunsgi

It is situated on a minor stream feeding River Krishna in the Gulbarga district of Karnataka. Hunsgi, along with the adjacent Baichbal Valley, has been a focus of intensive survey by K. Paddayya [1982]. He has examined the Palaeolithic remains in the region in the context of palaeo-environmental conditions. His studies have revealed a large number of

Acheulian sites having a variety of tools including choppers, cleavers, knives and scrapers made on the locally available raw material — limestone. Employment of both hard (stone) and soft (wooden or bone hammer) techniques is evident. A cluster of artifacts found near the limestone rocks indicate that tools were manufactured at the site and then carried to other areas. The discovery of a quarry site at Isampur in Hunsgi Valley in 1997 gives credence to this view. K. Paddayya identifies living quarters and base camps in the Hunsgi-Baichbal Valley and argues that the movement of people up and down was conditioned by the seasonal availability of food resources within the close proximity of their base camp. K. Paddayya's work on Hunsgi is treated as an important milestone in the field of Lower Palaeolithic studies in South Asia.

Inamgaon

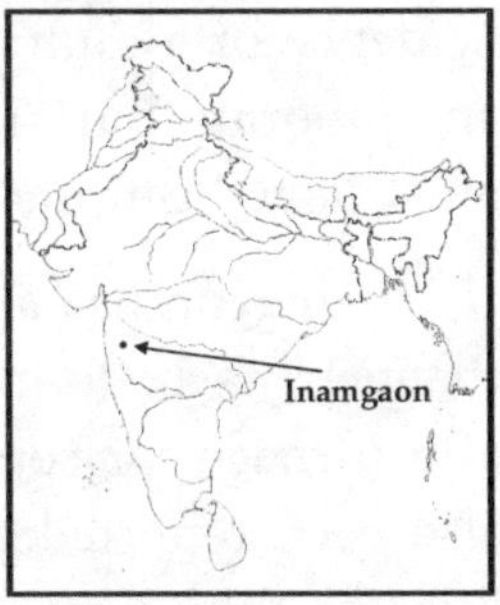

It is located on the right bank of the stream called Ghod, a tributary of the river Bhima, in Pune district of Maharashtra. The excavations have brought to light an extensive settlement of the Chalcolithic period ranging in date from 1600 BC – 700 BC. It is an important site of the Jorwe Culture. Dhavalikar, on the basis of detailed survey of the archaeological data, highlights the settlement-subsistence pattern of the people and infers the presence of a chiefdom society at Inamgaon.

In the initial phase (1600BC – 1400 BC) the people showed affinity with the Malwa culture. They lived in large rectangular houses having a *chulha* (hearth) and arrangements for storing food grains. The people subsisted on agriculture, hunting and fishing. They domesticated animals such as cattle, goat, sheep and pig, and used tools made of chalcedony as well as of copper, though the latter are scarce in number. Their principal ware was Black-on-Red painted ware.

Period II (1400 BC – 1000 BC) is marked by the features of Jorwe culture and shows greater progress over the earlier period. The houses were built with well-laid-out floor and indicate some attempt at planning. One of the houses had a channel dug outside in the courtyard to drain out rain water from the roof. There is also evidence of the houses of copper-smiths and potters. A structure with six pit silos of varying sizes with platforms has been identified as a granary. Adjoining to it is a big house consisting of five rooms. In the courtyard of this house has been found a burial containing a skeleton of a man in an urn. Dhavalikar believes that the evidence of a multi-roomed structure, a nearby granary and an elaborate burial, all indicate that the person in the urn must have been the ruling chief of the area.

Inamgaon has also revealed an embankment along with a channel, maybe to irrigate the neighbouring fields. The remains of a furnace for copper smelting and of a potter's kiln have also been reported. The dead were buried in a pit especially dug for the purpose. In the case of adults, the entire body was placed in the pit , but before doing so the portion below the ankle was chopped off — a practice not followed in the urn burial of the "chief" noted above, maybe because the dead occupied some special social or religious status. The discovery of clay figurines of females has led scholars to propose that the people of Inamgaon were the worshippers of mother-goddess.

The last phase at Inamgaon, after 1000 BC, was marked by decline, maybe as Dhavalkar argues, because of a change in climate which became arid and uncongenial. The overall degeneration is reflected in small dwellings and coarse pottery. The habitation was finally deserted around 700 BC.

Jakhera

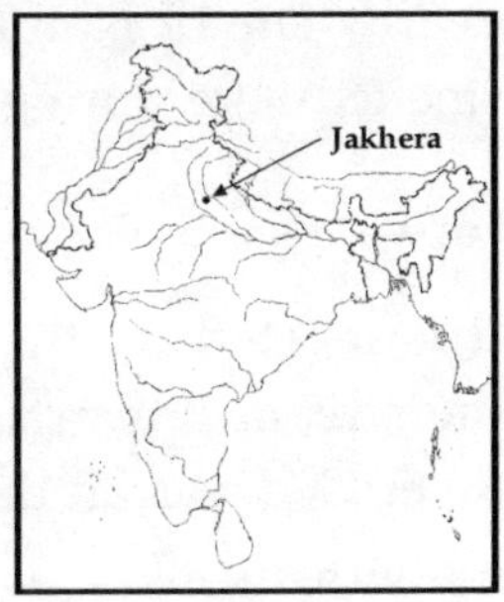

It is situated in district Etah in Western Uttar Pradesh. It is basically associated with the Painted Grey Ware Culture (1100 BC – 600 BC) and represents the growing use of iron in the agricultural activities in the Upper Gangetic Valley. The antiquities found here include large number of iron tools such as hoes, sickles and, most importantly, ploughshares, copper objects, mostly in form of ornaments, bone tools, gold objects, ivory objects such as pendants, beads of carnelian and other semi-precious stones. The evidence of slag and furnaces at Jakhera indicates local smelting of iron [Tripathi : 2001]. The people lived in wattle-and-daub houses containing underground storage pits. There are also some *kund*-like pits which may have been used for the purpose of some ritual activity [Chakrabarti : 1999: 259].

Jodhpura

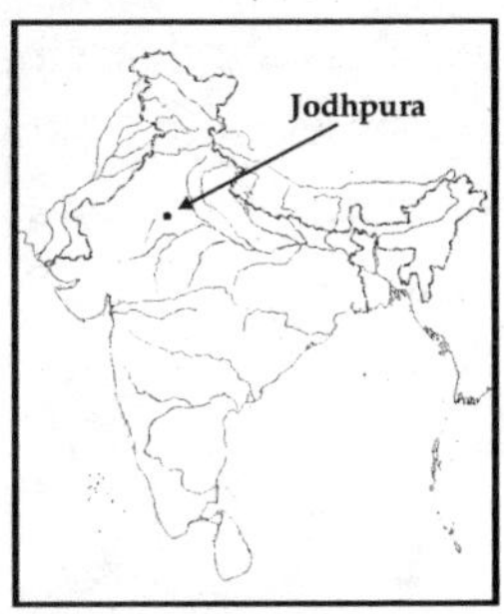

It is located in Jaipur district of Rajasthan. The excavations here have revealed a continuous growth of cultural activity over five different periods, starting with Ochre Coloured Ware (OCW) which is found at the lowest level and is dated to 2600 BC. This early date for OCP suggests that this pottery is almost contemporary with the Harappan civilization. It is found along with some bits of copper and terracotta beads. OCP level is followed in succession by the PGW (Painted Grey Ware) phase, associated with the use of iron implements and the NBPW phase. The presence of slag and furnaces at Jodhpura and the nearby site of Noh (Bharatpur) indicates that iron was being smelted here during the PGW period (1100 BC – 600 BC).

Jorwe

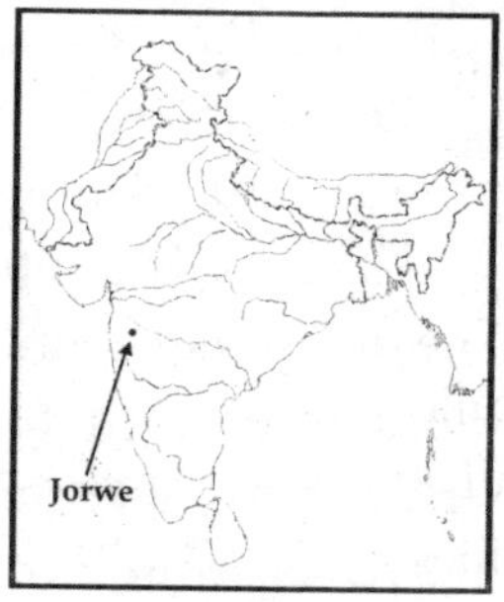

It is located on the northern bank of the stream Pravara, a tributary of the River Godavari in district Ahmadnagar, Maharashtra. The excavations conducted here by H.D. Sankalia in early 1950s brought to light a Chalcolithic Culture dating to mid second millennium BC. This discovery marked a new chapter in Indian archaeological research as it tended to bridge the gap between the decline of Harappa cities and the beginning of the early historical period — a subject which earlier posed a serious question. Jorwe has reported a typical Black-on-Red pottery, identified for the first time here, and hence designated as Jorwe Ware. This pottery is wheel-made, slipped and painted in black, the designs being mainly geometric in form, i.e., dots, circles, lines, etc. It is found in association with the copper axes and bangles. Today Black-on-Red pottery has been reported from many other sites in India, and going by radiometric dates, it is dated back to 2000 BC at some places [Settar and Korisettar (ed) : 2002: 181].

Kayatha

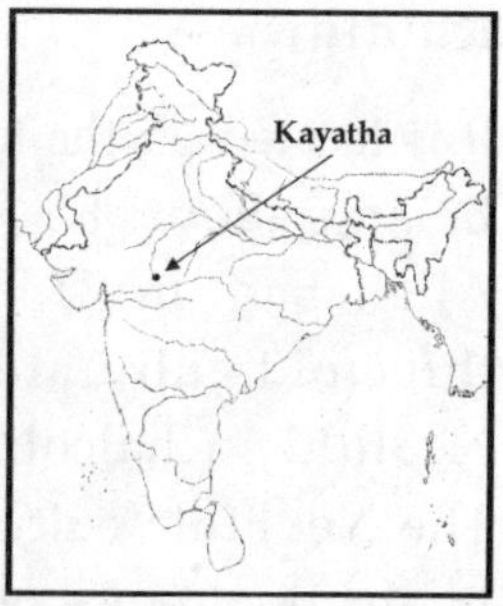

It is situated on the right bank of the stream Chotti Kali Nadi, a tributary of River Kali Sind, about 25 km east of Ujjain. It is predominantly a Chalcolithic site and the excavations conducted here by Wakankar have brought to light different phases of the Chalcolithic Culture. These phases, identified on the basis of pottery types, range from c. 2000 BC to 1200 BC (uncalibrated) though some antiquities of the historical period have also been noticed.

The earliest Chalcolithic phase is termed as Kayatha culture (c. 2000 BC – 1800 BC) on the basis of its distinctive pottery called Kayatha Ware which is fine and sturdy with dark brown slip and painted patterns in the form of loops and zig-zag lines. It is followed in succession by the pottery types used by the people of Banas (1700 BC – 1500 BC) and Malwa (1500 BC – 1200 BC).

The cumulative evidence as gathered from the archaeological data at Kayatha suggests that the Kayatha people lived in wattle and daub houses, and used stone as well as copper for their tools. An important find here is that of two fine axes cast in mould. About 28 bangles of copper, a large number of beads of agate and carnelian and about 40,000 microbeads of steatite, the largest number ever reported from any Chalcolithic site, have also been discovered. It indicates that copper and bead industry at Kayatha was highly developed. An interesting find here is that of typical terracotta bull figurines, most of which show the head with horns but no hind part. These stylized bulls have no parallels elsewhere and, as it is suggested, may have been used as votive offerings.

Koldihwa

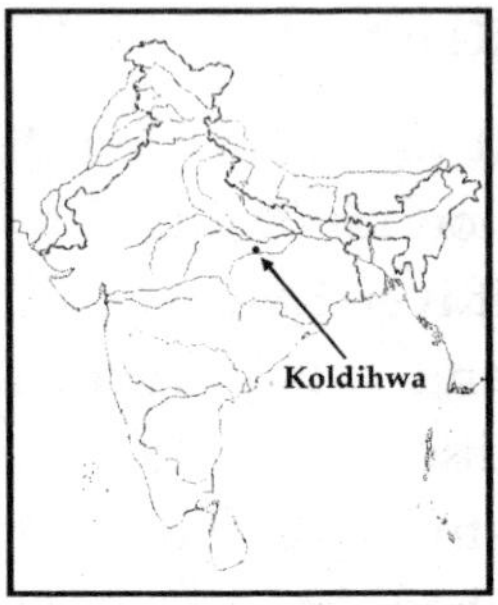

It is located on the left bank of the River Belan, about 85 km south-east of Allahabad in U.P. It has revealed threefold cultural sequence covering Neolithic, Chalcolithic and Iron Age. The Neolithic culture is distinguished by the occurrence of ground stone tools along with microliths and handmade ill-fired pottery with cord impression. The rice husk found embedded into the burnt clay pieces indicates the cultivation of rice. According to G.R. Sharma [1980] the C_{14} dates of the Neolithic levels from which the evidence of rice is obtained range between seventh to fifth millennium BC. He also argues that Koldihwa presents the earliest evidence of rice cultivation in the Indian subcontinent. But other scholars are skeptical about such an early date for rice in India and doubt the authenticity of the sample used for carbon dating.

The second level at Koldihwa is Chalcolithic, distinguished by the use of Black-and-Red Ware which is made on wheel and is of well-levigated clay. There is also evidence of use of copper axe and arrowhead. The discovery of iron crucibles and slag along with iron axe and arrowheads indicates the gradual adoption of iron technology by the people later on. Charred grains of wheat and *mung* show the introduction of new cultivated crops in addition to rice which continued as earlier.

Kuchai

It is located in Mayurbhanj district, north of the town of Baripada in Orissa. It is a site of Neolithic Culture explored and excavated in 1960s. It is distinguished by the presence of ground stone implements like axes and shouldered adzes. Other tools recovered here are microliths which lay below the Neolithic level and include blades, points and scrapers — all non-geometric in form. No structural remain has been reported so far. The age of the tool outfit at Kuchai still remains to be ascertained but on the basis of a comparative study of data from West Bengal, B.K. Thapar assigns it to the last quarter of the second millennium BC. It is pointed out that the main significance of the site lies in the sequence of two cultures — Microlithic and Neolithic, the former being identified for the first time in Orissa.

Kupgal or Kupgallu

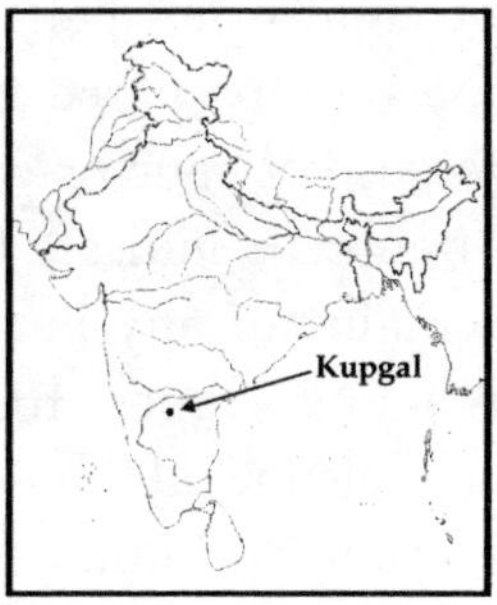

It lies slightly away from the River Tungabhadra, about 8 km east of district Bellary near the summit called the Peacock Hill in Karnataka. Robert Foote had earlier reported the presence of rock shelters and the vestiges of Neolithic habitation here. He had also identified a 'factory area' on the basis of scattered stone artifacts such as axes and chisels in various stages of fabrication. On the face of the hillock rock bruisings or engravings representing human and animal figures and hunting scenes were observed. It is believed that these engravings belong to the Neolithic phase and are thus later in time than the paintings at Bhimbetka. Kupgal also represents an ashmound site marked by the heaps of ash collected as a result of periodical burning of cattle dung. These mounds are associated with the Neolithic period. However, the nature of these ashmounds has been a matter of controversy. While Allchin associates them with the cattle camps of the Neolithic people, K. Paddayya considers them as habitational sites of the pastoralists.

Langhnaj

It is situated in Mehsana district, about 60 km north of Ahmedabad in Gujarat. It is a Mesolithic site excavated by, among others, H.D. Sankalia. The main microlithic tools found here include triangles, trapezes, lunates and scrapers. The raw material used for these tools is mainly chert, chalcedony and quartz which must have been brought from their source areas lying at some distance. The tools are prepared from cores through indirect percussion by the use of bone or wooden hammer. The charred bone remains of animals indicate the knowledge of fire and cooking but no remains of any hearth and ashes have been found. Pottery remains suggest that it was mostly handmade. Remains of animals include those of nilgai, cattle, deer, etc. About a dozen human skeletons lying in east-west (head towards east) orientation throw light on their burial practice. The burial goods include beads of shell which must have also been brought from the coastal area of Gujarat. The discovery of a copper knife in the levels of Mesolithic occupation is interesting as it indicates some direct or indirect contact with some contemporary copper-using culture. The identification of Mesolithic phase at Langhnaj is significant as it bridges the gap between the Palaeolithic and the Neolithic periods in Gujarat.

Mahadaha

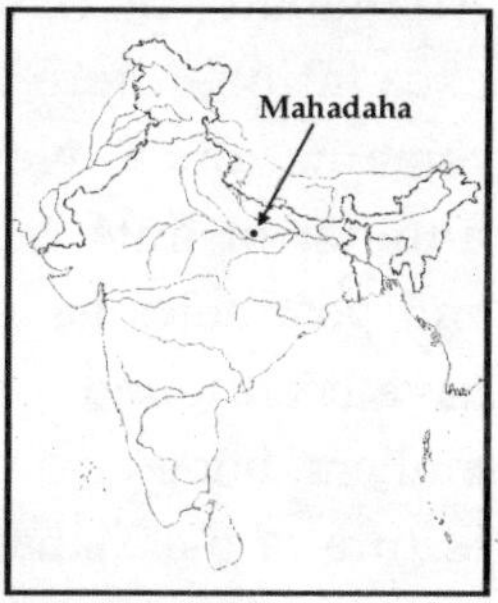

It is situated on the banks of an ancient oxbow or horseshoe lake about 31 km north-east of the town of Pratapgarh in Uttar Pradesh. It is a Mesolithic site dating back to 2850 BC (calibrated) [Chakrabarti : 1999: 106]. It has revealed three distinct areas — the habitation-cum-burial area, the butchering area (as identified by the scatter of bones of wild cattle), and the lake area. Among burials, there are two cases of twin burials in which a male and a female are put together — in one case the female is placed above the male, and in another they lie side by side. The grave goods include burnt animal bones, microliths, bone ornaments in the form of a necklace and a pendant.

The microliths are made of chert, chalcedony and agate. As this raw material for microliths is not available locally, it must have been brought from a distance of about 70-100 km from their source area in the Vindhyas, probably in exchange for some local product. Among all the Mesolithic sites, Mahadaha presents the best evidence for the use of bone and antler objects which are divided into three groups, viz., implements, ornaments and utensils [Sharma, G.R. : 1980: 107-09], and include arrowheads, blades, knives, rings, necklaces, etc. Mahadaha, as G.R. Sharma argues, furnishes a valuable evidence of the adaptability of Palaeolithic man to a particular habitat and ecology having limited stone.

Mahagara

It is situated in the Belan Valley, opposite another important site of Koldihwa, about 85 km south-east of Allahabad in Uttar Pradesh. The excavations here have yielded the remains of a Neolithic culture. A number of huts represented by floors and post-holes have been exposed. On the floor of huts there have been found a number of microliths, stone blades, querns, mullers, bone arrowheads and terracotta beads. A noteworthy feature of the Mahagara excavations is the discovery of a cattle pen area containing hoof impressions of cattle [Thapar, B.K.: 1987: 250]. The area was fenced and could accommodate fifty to sixty animals. The domesticated animals included cattle, sheep and goat. The people of Mahagara cultivated rice. It is evident from the rice husk found in the paste of the pottery. Mahagara excavations suggest that the Neolithic people of the area followed a mixed economy based on agriculture and cattle-herding.

Mahisdal

It is situated on the banks of a stream called Kopai in district Birbhum of West Bengal. Excavated in 1960s, it has revealed two cultural periods. Period I, which is more prominent, is Chalcolithic in nature, though copper implements are rare. C_{14} dates for this period range from 1400 BC to 900 BC. The impressions of reed on burnt clay indicate that the people lived in simple mud-plastered structures. The carbonised rice seeds recovered in bulk from a pit-granary suggest the cultivation of this crop. These rice seeds are believed to belong to a fine variety. While copper is scarce, stone and bone implements are prolific and appear to have been produced locally. There is evidence of the use of microliths including scrapers, lunates and points. It is pointed out that restricted use of copper was probably because of the non-availability of metal in close proximity of the site. The presence of beads of steatite and semi-precious stones, bangle pieces, decorated combs, etc., indicates the interest that people took in personal decoration. Among other finds, reference may be made to an object termed as "terracotta phallus." Whether it was connected with the religious belief of the people, one can't be sure. The Chalcolithic period on the whole represents a sedentary peasantry following a mixed agricultural and hunting-fishing life. A large conflagration is believed to have brought an end to the Chalcolithic life. The Chalcolithic phase was followed by Iron Age, represented by the occurrence of iron arrowheads, spearheads as well as a large quantity of rice.

Mahurjhari

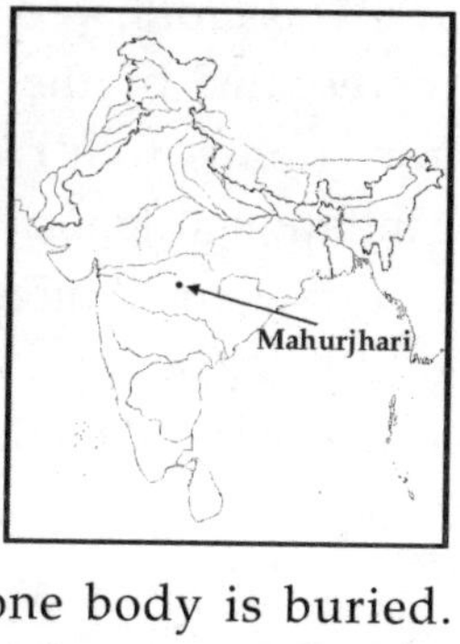

It lies 150 km west of Nagpur in the state of Maharashtra. It along with **Junapani**, which lies close to it, marks an important Megalithic site where a number of stone-circled burials of different dimensions have been found. These burials normally contain one skeleton but in some cases more than one body is buried. These burials have also yielded Black-and-Red Ware, objects of iron, copper and gold objects, etched and unetched beads of agate and carnelian. The iron tool-kit comprises flat rectangular axes, lances and spears. There have also been found horse face-masks (blinkers) of copper sheets with iron knobs rivetted to it.

Maski

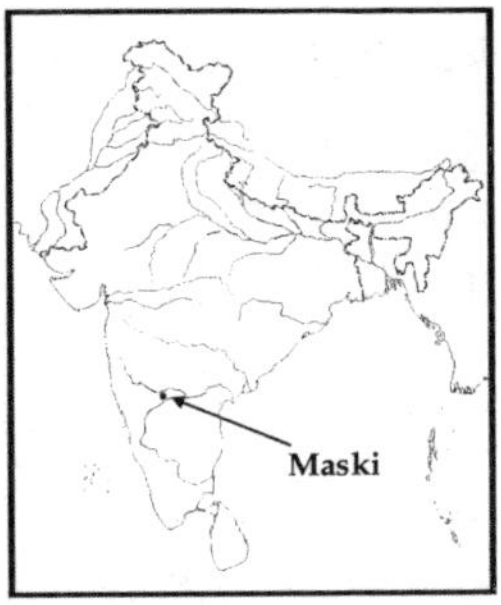

It is situated on a tributary of the River Tungabhadra in Raichur district of Karnataka. It has revealed a set of Asokan Minor Rock Edicts which significantly mention the name of Asoka as their author. Archaeologically, Maski is important for the remains of the Neolithic-Chalcolithic and the Megalithic Cultures.

Neolithic Culture dated to latter half of the second millennium BC is dominated by microliths and ground stone implements. The raw material used for them includes chert, agate and carnelian. Copper has a restricted presence. The pottery is mostly plain though there are also some painted pieces. Animal remains include those of sheep, goat and cattle.

It is followed by the Megalithic culture which is represented by the introduction of Black-and-Red Ware and iron. Iron is well represented in the burials as well as in the habitational deposits. The objects include lances, arrowheads and daggers. Among the beads of various materials, one of gold has also been found. The Megalithic period is assigned to the first millennium BC.

Mehrgarh

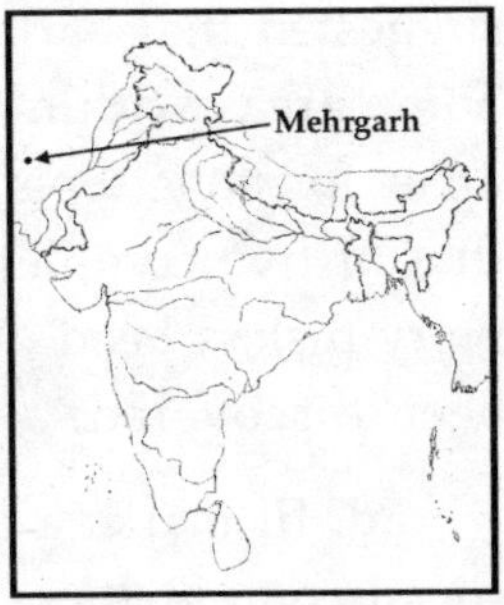

It is situated on the banks of the River Bolan in Kachi plains of Baluchistan, Pakistan. It has yielded the earliest evidence of agricultural activity based on wheat-barley cultivation and sheep-goat domestication in the Indian sub-continent. Initially, as Chakrabarti [1999, 117] points out, these activities were confined to a smaller area in Baluchistan but later they came to spread all over major areas in the neighbourhood. Excavated by Jarrige in 1970s and 1980s, Mehrgarh reveals a continuous cultural growth from 7000 BC to the beginning of the Harappan period. The sequence of growth has been divided into many periods and sub-periods, the chronology of which is "not clear-cut." Broadly it can be divided into three phases : 7000 BC – 6000 BC; 6000 BC – 5000 BC; 5000 BC – 3500 BC.

Mehrgarh is treated as a nuclear region for the cultivation of both wheat and barley. The evidence of crop cultivation in Pd. I comes from the charred remains as well as from the impression of wheat and barley on mud-bricks. A large number of animal bones recovered from the site indicate sheep-goat domestication, but there is limited bone tool industry. The human burials indicate bodies wearing personal ornaments, viz., necklaces made of shell, bone rings, and sometimes lapis lazuli beads, the last one indicating exchange or trade contact with the people far north in Afghanistan which contains lapis lazuli mines.

While Pd. I is aceramic, Pd. II is marked by the use of pottery, though it is handmade and is very limited. Some compartmented structures suggest storage of grains as seeds of barley have been reported from a few of them. It is suggested that barley was grown with the help of irrigation. Some areas within the site have been identified as working areas for bone tools and steatite objects. An important find is that of two complete sickles with inset microlithic tools. An ivory tusk, a bead of copper and small copper ingot have also been discovered.

Pd. III marks a great progress in craft activities leading to social complexities. A few terracotta crucibles with traces of copper suggest, for the first time, local copper-smelting though copper beads and rings have been reported from earlier periods too. There is also a large-scale production of wheel-made painted pottery. A number of storage units or granaries have been reported. This is also the period when terracotta humped bulls, so prominent in the Harappan Culture, first appear. An important feature noticed in the burial system is that sometimes more than one dead are placed together. Personal ornaments, mostly necklaces of steatite microbeads, but sometimes beads of lapis lazuli or carnelian too, are included among the grave goods. A study of the skeletons has revealed that in Pd. III people suffered more from dental problems such as caries and tooth loss which, as it is suggested, might have been because of change in food diet based more on cereals. Incidentally, as reported in the press recently (*The Hindu*, Delhi edn., April 23, 2006, p. 13, col. 1), a team of international scholars has found at Mehrgarh an evidence of the use of 'flint-tipped wooden drills' to cure dental diseases. This is supposed to be the earliest evidence of dental care in the world. Slowly and gradually, the life at Mehrgarh came to merge with the Harappan Civilization.

Naikund

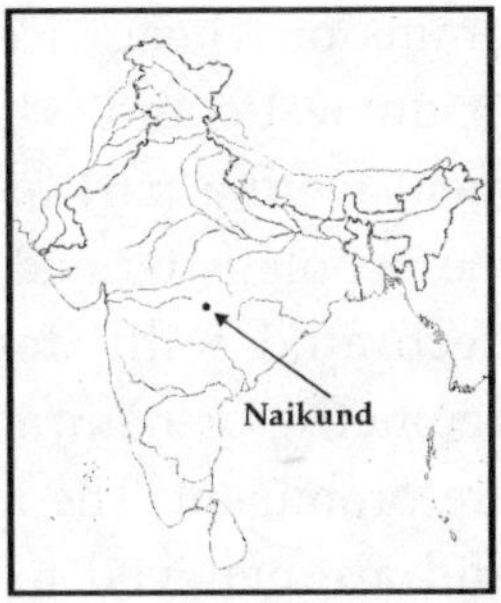

It lies 45 km north-east of Nagpur in the Vidarbha region of Maharashtra. It is a Megalithic habitation site and has yielded a number of stone-circle graves. The people lived in circular huts having wooden posts to support a thatched roof. The antiquities found here include iron daggers, spears, axes, Black-and-Red Ware as well as the charred grains of wheat, common pea, lentil and blackgram. The remains of horse and its copper ornaments have also been reported.

Naikund offers an important evidence of iron-smelting at the site. It is confirmed by the presence of the remains of a furnace built of curved bricks and a clay pipe for blowing in the air. Around the furnace is found iron slag and a fragmentary iron axe. In the opinion of S.B. Deo, Naikund came to be occupied first by the Megalithic people in around the seventh century BC.

Navadatoli

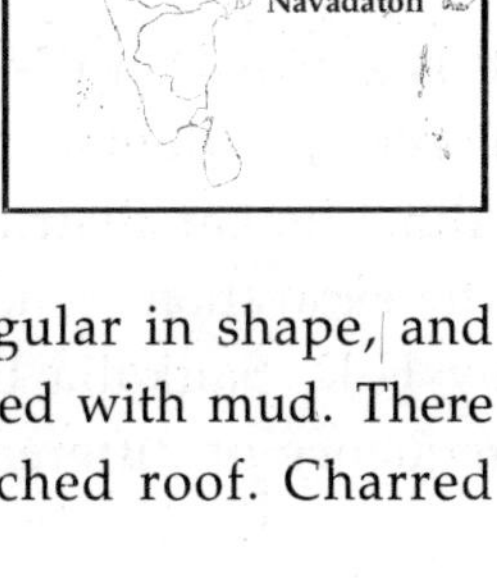

It is located on the southern bank of the River Narmada in district Nimar of Madhya Pradesh. Excavated by Sankalia in 1950s, it represents the chief Chalcolithic site of the Malwa Culture, though remains of Palaeolithic and NBPW are also recovered. It is dated to roughly 2000 BC – 1750 BC. The house structures were either circular or rectangular in shape, and were made of split bamboo screen plastered with mud. There were wooden posts to support the thatched roof. Charred grains of wheat, rice, legumes, oil seeds as well as the bones of domestic and wild animals indicate that both cereals and meat were a part of their food. The distinct pottery used by the people is termed as Malwa ware. It is orange slipped ware decorated with designs in black. The designs are either geometric or naturalistic, among the latter animals and birds are prominent. The microlithic tools (lunates etc.,) are plentiful, and are believed to have been produced locally. Stone was also used to produce querns and pestles. Navdatoli has also yielded copper flat-axes, bangles, fish-hooks and a broken mid-ribbed sword. An analysis of the specimens has revealed that copper was alloyed with both tin and lead indicating an advanced copper technology. Ornaments in the form of beads, earrings and bangles were made of diverse material such as copper, shell and terracotta.

Navdatoli throws some interesting sidelight on the religious beliefs of the people. The pit found dug in the centre of a house has been taken to represent a *kund* for fire worship. Similarly, a jar decorated with the figures of a female and a lizard with what looks like a "shrine" between the two has led Dhavalikar to argue that the "shrine" is that of a deity associated with the alligator. Incidentally, Navdatoli literally means a village of boatmen among whom alligator occupies an important position.

Nevasa

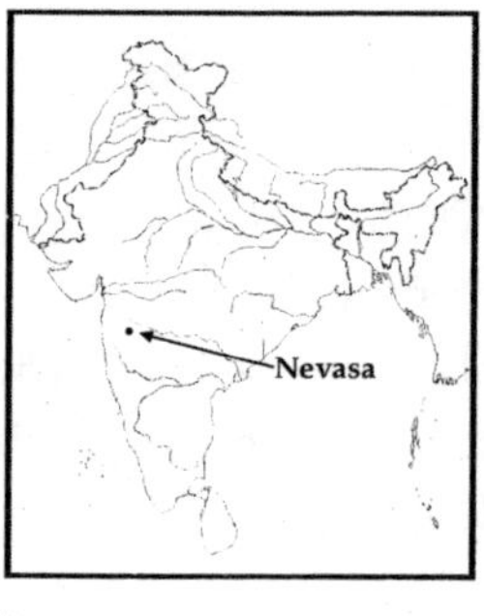

It is situated on the banks of the River Pravara, a tributary of the Godavari, in Ahmadnagar district of Maharashtra. The excavations conducted here in 1950 by H.D. Sankalia brought to light a sequence of different cultural periods ranging from the Lower Palaeolithic to the Chalcolithic to the Medieval times. Later in 1960s and 1970s Corvinus excavated the nearby site called **Chirki-Nevasa** to distinguish the location from the one excavated by Sankalia.

Earliest phase here is represented by Palaeolithic or Acheulian tools which include chopper-chopping tools, hand-axes, cleavers, etc., According to Corvinus, a heavy concentration of finished and unfinished tools at the site suggests that it was a location of the workshop for Acheulian tools. He has also unravelled an occupation floor of the Lower Palaeolithic Culture. The next cultural phase is marked by the presence of distinct Middle Palaeolithic tools. It is represented by flakes tools and other tool-types such as points, scrapers and borers which indicate a clear evolution from the preceding Lower Palaeolithic phase. The dwelling structures with plastered floors and wooden posts appear in the Chalcolithic phase, dated from 1500 BC – 1000 BC. There is evidence of the use of wheel-made pottery, called Jorwe ware, having designs in geometric pattern. *Chulahs* as well as huge storage jars with tapering bottoms to fix them in the floors have also been noticed. The beads and bangles made of copper have been found in the burials.

Noh

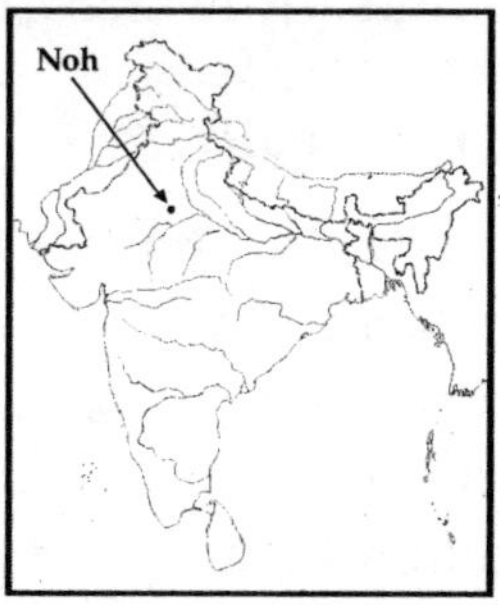

It is situated in the district of Bharatpur, Rajasthan. It, like Jodhpura (Jaipur Distt.), has revealed five different cultural phases of growth beginning with Ochre Coloured Pottery (OCP). Its PGW levels have reported iron spearheads, axes and also, most importantly, rice, whereas the NBPW phase has yielded uninscribed cast coins along with mud brick structures and iron and copper objects. In the Sunga-Kushan period there appear baked brick structures, hearths, shell bangles, etc.

Paisra

It lies in the Kharagpur region of eastern India. It has revealed a working floor for the Palaeolithic and Mesolithic tools. The entire area was found extremely rich in finished and semi-finished tools, cores, flakes and chips belonging to the Palaeolithic period. The presence of big and small fire places at the site indicates that stone was probably heated before flaking. A series of post-holes to uphold the thatched roof indicate some sort of habitation by the Palaeolithic people. The Mesolithic layers at the site have yielded lunates and scrapers. But there is limited evidence of Mesolithic habitation. It has led the excavators to suggest that people probably did not occupy this place for a long time as no organic remains in the form of cereals or animal bones have been reported. The significance of Paisra lies in the fact that it provides the earliest evidence of a Mesolithic site belonging to the seventh millennium BC in the eastern part of India [Chakrabarti : 1999: 110].

Paiyampalli

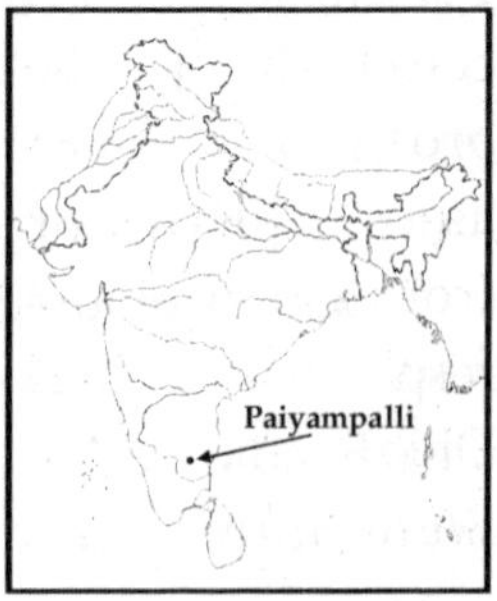

It is a site situated in the north Arcot region of Tamil Nadu. The excavations conducted here in 1960s have revealed an overlap of Neolithic with Megalithic cultures. The lower levels have yielded Neolithic tools and implements whereas the upper levels contain Mesolithic Black-and-Red ware and the related antiquities.

The tools of the Neolithic period consist of bone and stone implements, former being represented by points and scrapers, and the latter by stone blades, mace-heads and axes. Querns, pestles, pounders have also been found. No metal is reported in the Neolithic levels. In the Megalithic period, however, iron is used profusely for making sickles, knives, spearheads, arrowheads, etc. The use of gold ornaments by the Megalithic people is attested by the recovery of a stone mould of a goldsmith. The beads of semi-precious stones and shell have also come to light. The Megalithic people lived in circular or long houses of thatched roof supported by wooden posts. Their burials consisted of stone-circles, and these have revealed a deposit of iron weapons and Black-and-Red pottery. The subsistence economy of the people during both Neolithic and Mesolithic periods appears to be agriculture and cattle rearing, supplemented by hunting and fishing. The radiocarbon dates of Megalithic phase at Paiyampalli range from seventh century BC to fourth century BC.

Pandu Rajar Dhibi

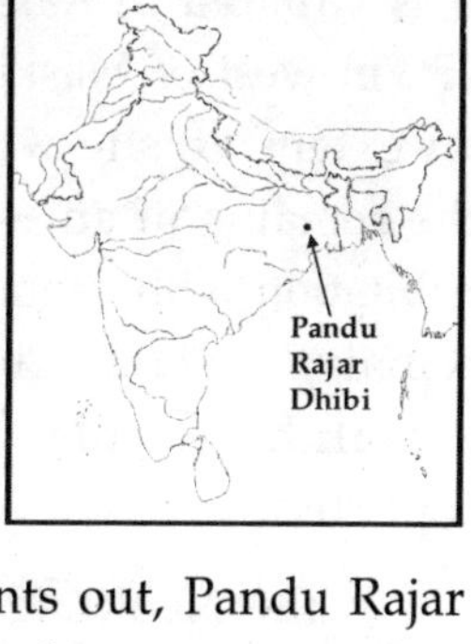

It is situated in the flood plains of the River Ajay in district Burdwan of West Bengal. The large-scale excavations conducted here in 1960s have revealed broadly three distinct cultural phases associated with Chalcolithic Culture, Iron Age and Early Historical Period, respectively. As Chakrabarti [1999: 24] points out, Pandu Rajar Dhibi is the first multicultural site to have been excavated in West Bengal and its earliest phase may go back to 1500 BC.

In the Chalcolithic period, people lived in mud huts with thatched roof supported by bamboo posts. Hearths were used for cooking. The evidence of charred rice seeds and impression of paddy husks on the pottery are indicative of cultivation and consumption of rice. Remains of the bones which have been identified are those of humped cattle, pig, nilgai and sambhar. Some of these were domesticated while others were utilized as food. Antlers were used for fashioning bone tools such as awls and arrowheads. Pottery was initially coarse but later improved and contained painted motifs in the form of geometric designs such as dots, dashes, criss-cross and wavy lines. Copper objects such as fish-hooks, bangles, rings and beads of semi-precious stones, sometimes etched, were also recovered. The following iron phase was marked by progress in pottery making. A noteworthy find of this period is a structure with six elliptical ovens containing iron slag and a broken blade of iron. It clearly suggests that iron was smelted at the site. Another important find here is that of a gold coin of king Kanishka I (first century AD).

Piklihal

It is situated in Raichur district, about 25 km west of Maski in Karnataka. It is an extensive site where Allchin noted the remains of an essentially Neolithic habitation with ashmound. The material remains related to the iron-using megalith people have also been reported.

In the Neolithic period, which is divided into early and later phases, people domesticated cattle, sheep and goat and cultivated millet and pulses. They used hearths for cooking and saddle querns for grinding. There is also some evidence of the use of copper for bowls. Neolithic-Chalcolithic period overlaps with the Megalithic Culture which is marked by the use of Black-and-Red Ware and iron objects such as sickle, knife and arrowheads.

Piklihal has also revealed rock-paintings, bruisings and engravings on the hillock. These paintings are mostly in red ochre and depict, besides animals, dancing human figures, and belong to Prehistorical as well as Historical periods.

Sanaganakallu

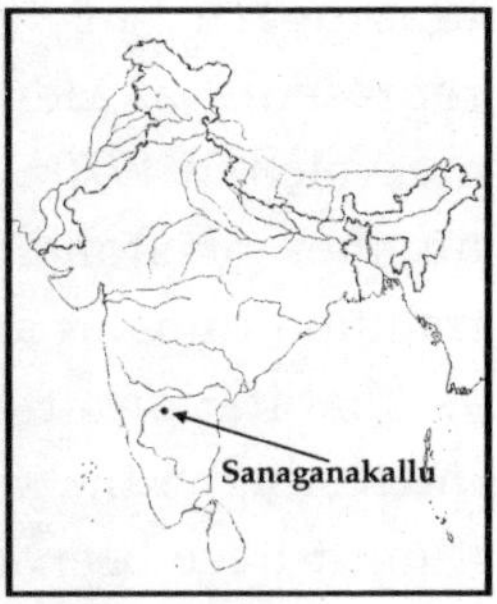

It is situated 5 km north-east of the town of Bellary in Karnataka. Excavated in 1960s, it has brought to light a cultural sequence from the Palaeolithic to the Neolithic and has also yielded the Chalcolithic and Megalithic material remains. The hills of the area contain a number of rock bruisings or sketches depicting figures of men, animals and birds.

Palaeolithic period is represented by chopper-chopping tools and flake tools. It is followed by a microlithic industry of the Mesolithic phase marked by quartz flakes and lunates. The Neolithic phase reveals houses having circular floors with post-holes at the edge to support the roof above. The stone tools which belong to this phase are axes, chisel and blades, and these are made on chert and chalcedony. The beginning of the Neolithic is dated to c. 1600 BC.

The Megalithic evidence is found overlapping with the Neolithic culture and is marked by the use of Black-and-Red Ware. Also discovered at Sanganakallu are the ashmounds containing heaps of burnt cattle dung. Robert Foote for the first time associated these ashmounds with the Neolithic culture. Later, Allchin suggested that these were cattle-camps of the Neolithic people. Recently, K. Paddayya has argued that these were habitation sites of the sedentary pastoral people. The debate on the nature and character of the ashmound is still on.

Sarai Nahar Rai

It is situated 15 km south-west of Pratapgarh in Uttar Pradesh. It represents a Mesolithic site which, excavated in 1970s, has revealed a large number of stone tools of geometric tradition (lunates and trapezes) as well as habitation floors and burials. Interestingly, the stone is not available locally, and therefore it must have been brought from distant areas in the Vindhya hills, may be in return for some local goods. The people lived around a lake with a horse-shoe form. It is believed that in Prehistoric times when this site was existing, the lake must have been large enough to provide hospitable conditions to many animals such as bison, rhino, stag and others whose bones have been discovered at the site.

The habitation at Sarai Nahar Rai is indicated by paved floors with post-holes to fix the poles to uphold the thatched roof. A number of hearths of different shapes (circular or oblong) and varied dimensions have also been noticed. A large hearth with a paved floor has been identified by the excavators as a community hearth. The burials at the site indicate that the dead were put in extending position, i.e., body resting on back. An interesting feature of the Sarai Nahar Rai burials is that, invariably, one of the hands of the dead is placed across the abdomen [Sharma, G.R.: 1980: 113]. In one skeleton a microlith has been found embedded in the body indicating a violent death.

Savalda

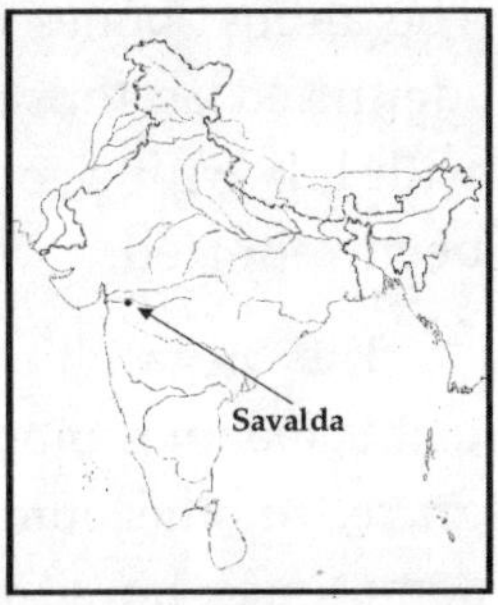

It is situated on the left bank of the River Tapti, about 20 km north-east of Nandurbar in district Dhulia of Maharashtra. Excavated in 1960s, it has revealed an occupational deposit belonging to the Chalcolithic and the NBPW periods, though later on some Palaeolithic material was also reported. The Chalcolithic phase revealed among other things a typical Black-painted Red Ware which came to be designated as Savalda ware. It is of medium to coarse fabric and contains painted motifs primarily of linear or geometric pattern such as lines, loops and circles. It is in the later period, Period II, that Black-and-Red Ware appears and the earlier pottery disappears. It may be noted that the so-called Savalda ware was not confined to the Tapti-Godavari Valley and has been reported from other parts in south India too. Its time-period goes back to 2000 BC, which may suggest some contact with the Late Harappan people.

Takalghata

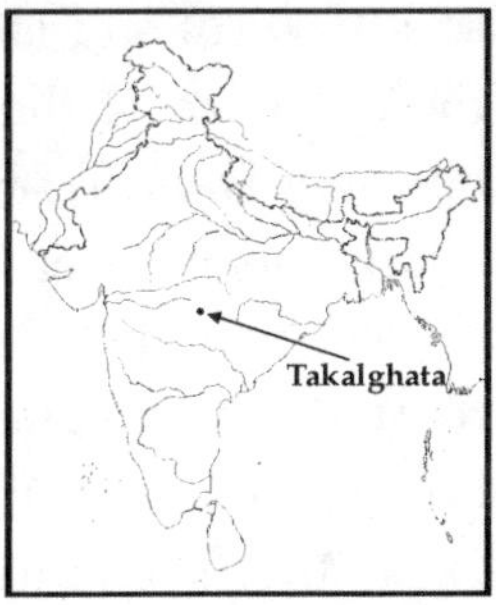

It lies 32 km west of Nagpur in the state of Maharashtra. It, along with Khapa which lies close to it, marks an important Megalithic site of the Vidarbha region. Takalghata is a habitation site whereas Khapa is a burial site. The excavations have revealed the presence of typical Megalithic pottery, i.e., Black-and-Red Ware with graffiti. Its shapes include bowls, lids and dishes. There is also evidence of etched and unetched beads of carnelian and agate. The iron artifacts include flat axes and daggers. The animal bones encountered in the excavations have been identified as those of cattle, pig and horse. Copper dishes with lids with a top having motifs of perched birds have also been reported.

The Megalithic burials at the nearby site of Khapa reveal that sometimes more than one person were buried in the same grave. Another interesting feature of the Khapa burials is that sometimes horse along with its face-mask (blinkers) and mounting gadgets was also buried by the side of the dead. The date assigned to the Megalithic Culture in central India is around seventh-sixth century BC.

Tekkalakota

It is located in the Bellary district of Karnataka, south India. Excavated by Nagaraja Rao in 1960s, it is predominantly a Neolithic-Chalcolithic site with some remains of the Megalithic period. The Neolithic culture has been divided into two phases — early (1700 BC – 1600 BC) and later (1600 BC – 1500 BC), the later one having the evidence of the use of copper. Tekkalakota has revealed not only well-preserved foundations of circular huts but also a large quantity of faunal remains including those of domestic cattle, sheep and deer. Charred bones indicate that meat was roasted. There is no evidence of cereals but the cultivation of horsegram is attested. The artifacts recovered in the excavations include copper implements and gold ear-ornaments, beads of steatite and semi-precious stones, besides microliths (lunates and trapezes) made on chert and chalcedony, and ground and polished axes. Bone tools consist of scrapers, points and borers. Antlers were also used as tools. The rock shelters near the site contain petroglyphs (rock-carvings) depicting bulls, dogs and humans. It is pointed out that Neolithic-Chalcolithic Culture of Tekalakota exhibits some affinity with the Chalcolithic Cultures of central India and the Deccan.

Utnur

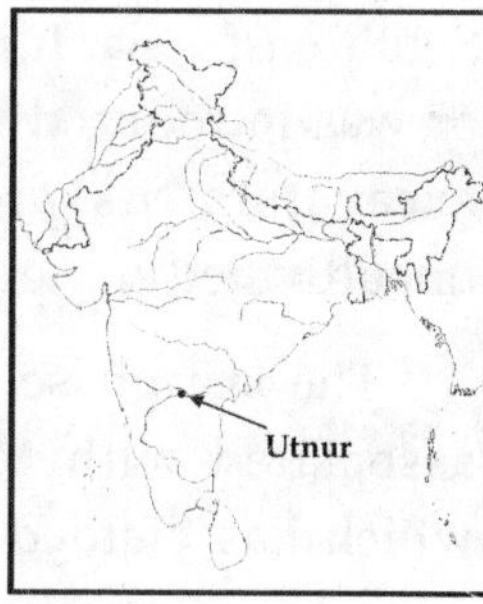

It is located in Andhra Pradesh, south India. It is an ashmound site of the Neolithic people, ranging in date from 2300 BC – 1250 BC. It has revealed a cattle pen area with imprints of cattle hoof marks. Allchin, who excavated the site in 1950s, believes that the size of the cattle pen area was big enough to accommodate 500 to 800 heads of cattle [1963: 156-63]. The ashmounds which were created on account of repeated burning of the cattle-dung have revealed no human habitational remains but have yielded potsherds and cattle bones, besides numerous stone tools such as flakes, blades, lunates and axes made on chert and jasper.

Watgal

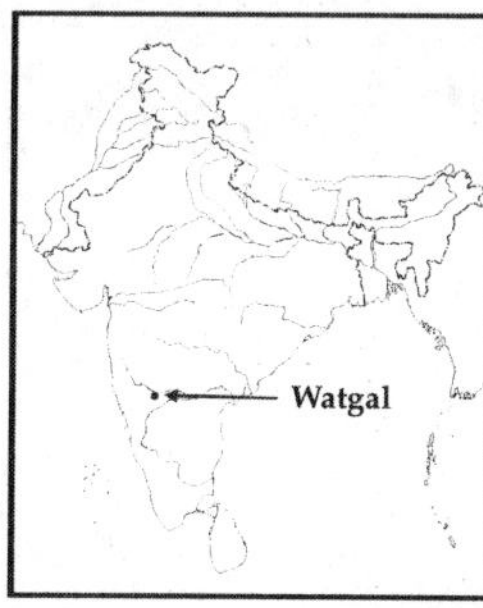

It is situated in the Raichur Doab, Karnataka. Though predominantly a Neolithic site, it represents a continuous cultural sequence from the Mesolithic to the Iron Age. It is the earliest non-ashmound Neolithic site yet documented, with the calibrated dates ranging from 2900 BC – 2600 BC. The radiocarbon determinations for Watgal, thus, push back the beginning of south Indian Neolithic by about 500 years. It has reported the oldest stone covered burial in south India, dated to 2700 BC – 2300 BC. It also provides the first evidence of an urn-burial in south. The recovery of shell artifacts at Watgal throw some light on the possible trade contact with coastal areas. Particularly intriguing is a reported find of areca nuts from a storage pit. It is today a widely prevalent stimulant chewed by people throughout India and South-East Asia. It is not clear whether it was native to Watgal or was introduced from outside, though, in the opinion of the excavators, its presence as a locally available wild and uncultivated variety cannot be ruled out.

The last phase at Watgal, dated to 1500 BC (calibrated), is associated with Megalithic stone chamber graves, one of which has yielded a small fragment of gold-wrapped silver wire and a number of vessels of Black-and-Red Ware with beads of copper.

Glossary

Accelerated Mass Spectometry (AMS)

A mechanism used in Radiocarbon dating. It needs as little as one gram of carbon or 0.5 gram of bone to calculate carbon-14, which is otherwise too small and unsuitable for the traditional C_{14} dating.

Acheulian (Acheulean)

It refers to a tool-making tradition characterized by stone handaxes and cleavers used in the Early Palaeolithic period. It takes its name from the site of St. Acheul in France where such tools were first noticed. Acheulian tools are basically core tools obtained by large flaking. These are an improvement over the earlier tool-making technique called Abbevillian (named after the place Abbeville, also in France) which produced crude and massive handaxes.

Ahar Culture

A Chalcolithic Culture dated to the second millennium BC. It is named after the chief site of Ahar in Rajasthan. It is also known as the Banas Culture after the river of the same name. It is characterised by greater use of copper in comparison to any other contemporary culture.

Antennae Sword

A sword with the hilt bifurcating like the antennae of insects.

It is a distinctive feature of the "Copper Hoard Cultures" dated to the 2nd millennium BC.

Anthropomorph

A figure representing human form. It is a distinctive feature of the "Copper Hoard Cultures" dated to second millennium BC.

Antler

It is a solid, bony horn of a male deer or of related animals having one or more branches. Antlers are shed once a year and grow back again during the next year. These were used by early humans for their tools and ornaments.

Archaeology

A study of human past as revealed in the material remains such as tools, weapons, household articles, ornaments, buildings, burials, etc.

Artifact (Artefact)

Any object of stone, wood or metal shaped or fashioned by man for his use. An analysis of the changing artefactual techniques may furnish an important insight into the behavioural pattern of a particular group of people.

Ashmound

It is a characteristic feature of the South Indian Neolithic Cultures, and refers to mounds formed by repeated burnings and accumulation of cattle dung in cattle pen areas. The precise reason for the burning remains unclear. The material found in the ash includes cattle bones, stone axes, blades, etc.

Assemblage

A set of artifacts, not necessarily of the same type, recovered from a specific archaeological site indicating its association with a particular cultural group.

Bifacial

A stone tool worked on both front and back faces or sides to form a cutting edge.

BP or bp

It is an abbreviated form of "Before Present"; the "present" is defined as CE 1950, the year when radiocarbon technique came to be introduced in dating archaeological remains. The term is used in contrast to BC or AD to signify the time-period.

Black-and-Red Ware

A type of ceramic found at various sites throughout India during the first and second millennium BC. It is black inside upto the rim and is red on the outer surface. It is believed that this colour effect was provided by putting the pot upside down in the kiln. This pottery was the chief characteristic feature of the Megalithic people of south India. It has also been reported from north India extending from Rajasthan to West Bengal. Because of its wide distribution and a long time-range, it cannot be attributed to a single cultural tradition.

Black-on-Red Ware

Pottery of red colour with paintings in black.

Blade

It refers to a long, thin flake of hard stone such as flint. It is different from a simple flake in the sense that it is twice as large as it is wide and has almost parallel sides. It was a prominent tool of the Upper Palaeolithic period and was produced from a carefully prepared core. Blade could also serve as a blank from which other artifacts such as burins or scrapers could be produced.

Burin

A pointed tool made of chipped flint which could be used for making hole in bone, antler, ivory or wood. It was an important hallmark of the Upper Palaeolithic period.

Celt

A hand tool in the form of a chisel or axe or adze of stone or any other material. It has a squared and bevelled (sloping), surface used for shaping wood or stone. It could be ground and polished to get sharper and smoother edge. It is of various varieties, such as bar celt, shouldered celt, etc.

Chalcolithic (Greek *khalkos*-copper; *lithos*-stone)

It refers to the period which followed the Neolithic phase, when copper implements came to be used along with stone tools. Normally, it also covers the Bronze Age. The Chalcolithic period marks a greater progress in social and economic life of the people in comparison to the earlier periods.

Chiefdom

It refers to a social organisation in which a chief along with some high ranking individuals close to him such as warriors occupy greater wealth and status in society than others. This disparity may be reflected in more lavish artifactual assemblages in and around the chief's house (which is normally bigger than other structures) and also in his grave goods. Chiefdoms often have a fortified area with a ritual centre and some degree of craft activity.

The chiefdom alongwith **band** (a small egalitarian group of hunters and gatherers who move regularly to obtain wild resources) and **tribe** (mobile pastoralists or settled groups with limited agriculture) are pre-state societies. A state is distinguished by such features as well-organised revenue system, bureaucratic administration, military power, etc.

Chopper-Chopping tools

A tool tradition followed in earlier phase of the Lower Palaeolithic period. These tools were prepared on pebbles by direct hitting on the edge. When it is flaked on one side, it is "unifacial" and is called "chopper," and when it is flaked on both sides, it is "bifacial" and is termed as "chopping tool." Together, these tools represent one single tool tradition.

Cleaver

An early Stone Age tool with a wide chisel edge. It could be used for cutting tree or any other material.

Copper-Hoards

A term used for convenience for hoards of copper objects found accidentally from different parts of northern India, but primarily from western Uttar Pradesh. The copper objects include anthropomorphic figures, harpoons, celts, swords, etc. They are dated to the second millennium BC and are normally associated with the people using Ochre Coloured Pottery (OCP). Their authorship is, however, a matter of debate.

Core

A piece of stone from which flakes are removed by striking it with another stone or hammer.

Cultural Evolution

It is a term which is basically used as a synonym for human progress and development. In the nineteenth century Thompsen, a Danish scholar, presented "Three Age System," i.e., Stone, Copper and Iron Age, to indicate a unilinear progress. Since 1950s, the progress is viewed more from the perspective of social change in association with biological evolution of human species. Thus, there is greater focus on emphasizing the progress from hunting-gathering stage to that of food production and surplus production. Leslie White views cultural progress in the context of different stages of growth from band, tribe and chiefdom to state.

Culture

In archaeological context, it refers to the artifacts or material remains having definite similarity representing the work of a particular group of people.

Culture History

A term which has come to be used since 1960s to describe the "traditional" attitude of collection and narration of excavated material remains in contrast to the study of "cultural process" as proposed by New or "processual" archaeologists.

Culture Sequence

The stages of cultural development as noticed in different layers of the material remains found in an archaeological excavation. The lowest layer is treated as the oldest in date.

Diffusion

It refers to a process of cultural change as a result of outside contact, physical or ideological, through trade, migration or even matrimonial relations. It overlooks the importance of internal factors in the matter of growth and change. It was widely followed by "culture historians" and is now being critised by the processual archaeologists who view change as a process involving many factors including local environment.

Ecofacts

Non-artifactual remains which have cultural relevance, i.e., faunal or floral material as well as soil and sediments.

Environmental Archaeology

A field in which archaeologists with the help of ecologists study the changes in ancient environment (palaeo-environment) to explain their impact on plants and animals. It also analyses the impact of environmental changes on the behavioural pattern of early humans.

Epipalaeolithic

A loosely defined chronological classification applied to the cultures which are technologically Palaeolithic in nature but represent its survival in later period. Sometimes it is used to refer to a stage between the Palaeolithic and the Mesolithic when microliths, the chief characteristic feature of the Mesolithic age, had not yet appeared.

Ethnoarchaeology

It refers to the study of behaviour and life pattern of the contemporary social groups, particularly the tribes, to understand and explain the factors which underlie the use and manufacture of Prehistoric tools and structures. The term coined by J.W. Fewkes in 1900 is an important element of the "processual archaeology."

Flake

A piece of stone chipped out of a core or a block. It could be retouched further to produce a sharp or tiny tool of a desired shape.

Flint

A hard but brittle stone, chemically quartzite. It can be flaked in any direction to acquire a desired shape. It occurs widely and was used as a basic material by man for his tool-kit until the advent of metal.

Flotation

A method of screening or sieving excavated material remains in water so as to separate and recover small seeds of grain or related objects.

Fossils

The remains, impressions or traces of any living organism found preserved in ancient rocks or sediments.

Gender Archaeology

A branch of archaeological studies that aims to highlight the specific role and contribution of females in different areas of activity (hunting, agriculture, crafts, etc.) as may be evident from the past remains. It tends to view the relationship between two sexes in a social rather than sexual or biological context and emphasizes that woman is capable of performing many more roles than just reproducing and rearing up children. It emerged in Europe in 1980s in response to feminist critiques who argued that archaeological studies were male biased or androcentric.

Geoarcheology

The use of geological methods and concepts to explain and understand the archaeological data related to metals and minerals, fossils, etc. The principle of "stratigraphic succession" which is the core of archaeological excavation is borrowed from geology.

Glacial or Glaciation

A term given to a period of earth's history when a large part of the world surface was covered with ice-sheets or glaciers. The less colder period between the two glacials, caused by the periodical melting of snow, is called inter-glacial which was marked by the growth of plant and animal life.

Hand-Axe

A characteristic stone tool of the Palaeolithic period. It was made by removing flakes from the core in such a way that one end of the core was given a point with sharp cutting edges leading down to it, and the other end was left rounded so as to fit conveniently into the palm of the hand, and hence its name.

Harpoon

It could be made of bone, antler or even metal, and comprised barbed (backward facing projection as in an arrow or a fish-hook), pointed head and a barbed shaft. It could be used for killing or catching fish. Its use became prominent in the Upper Palaeolithic period.

Holocene (Greek, *holos* — whole, *kainos* — recent)

It is a geological period that followed the Pleistocene age (ice-age) and extends upto the present. It began around 12,000/

10,000 BP and ushered in a warm and wet climate which led to profound changes in the subsistence patterns of early humans.

Hominid

The primates or mammals having the characteristic of a man; man is the only hominid extant.

Industry

In archaeological context it refers to an assemblage of tools and other artefacts of similar kind found from the same cultural layer. Hence the terms such as stone industry or bone industry.

Inhumation

Burial in the ground, as opposed to cremation.

k.y.a.

Abbreviation for "kilo years ago," i.e., a thousand years ago.

Levallosian

A special technique of tool-making which developed in the mid-Palaeolithic period. The technique involved first trimming of core and preparing a flat "tortoise" shaped platform, and then striking at the platform to produce symmetrical flakes. These flakes could be further retouched to give a desired shape. It marks a great progress over the earlier core-based Acheulean tools and demonstrates early human's planning and foresight. It derives its name from the site of Levallois in France where such tools were first noticed.

m.y.a.

An abbreviaiton for "million years ago," i.e., 1,000,000 years ago.

Madrasian

A name given to the Early Palaeolithic Cultures of south India. It is characterised by the presence of Acheulean type bifacial hand-axes and cleavers. Since these tools were reported first from Pallavaram near Madras, now Chennai, they came to be termed as "Madrasian."

Maritime Archaeology or Underwater Archaeology

A branch of archaeological study which aims to locate the past material remains under the sea, as against on the land, by identifying submerged coastal habitations, ship-wrecks, etc. This study, in recent years, has been greatly facilitated by the introduction of such devices as SONAR, which is used for detecting and locating objects underwater by the reflection of sound waves, and SCUBA (Self Contained Underwater Breathing Apparatus) which helps divers to stay longer under the sea.

Megalithic (Greek, *megas* — big; *lithos* — stone)

It refers to burial or commemorative monuments characterized by the use of large undressed or roughly dressed stones. These are of various types such as cists, dolmen, menhirs, etc. These are reported from different parts of the Indian subcontinent but are more prominent in south India. The Megalithic Cultures are characterised by the use of iron tools and Black-and-Red ware. They belong primarily to the first millennium BC.

Mesolithic (Greek, *mesos* — middle; *lithos* — stone)

It refers to the Middle Stone Age (not to be confused with Middle Palaeolithic period) and marks a phase of transition from the Palaeolithic to the Neolithic period. It coincides with the coming of Holocene Age around 10,000 BP when the climate became more congenial. It is characterised by the use of microliths or tiny geometric tools in the shape of triangles, trapezes, crescents, etc., which could be hafted in wooden or bone handles to form a 'composite tool.' There is also evidence of animal domestication, as a prelude to agricultural activity, in some regions during this period.

Microliths (Greek, *mikros* — small; *lithos* — stone)

It refers to tiny tools made on fine-grained stones like chalcedony, jaspar and agate by careful flaking. On the basis of their shapes, these are classified in two categories, viz., non-geometric comprising burins, borers and points, and geometric, having the shapes of triangles, trapezes or crescents. The geometric tools could be hafted in wooden or bone handle to serve as a sickle or a saw. The evidence from certain sites has revealed that geometric type of tools evolved gradually out of the non-geometric tradition.

Millennium

A period of thousand years. For example, in the context of pre-Christian era second millennium will be from 2000 BC – 1000 BC, and similarly, third millennium from 3000 BC – 2000 BC.

Neolithic (Greek, *neos* — new; *lithos* — stone)

It refers to the last phase of the Stone Age and was characterised by the use of ground and polished stone tools. But more than that it is defined in terms of better subsistence economy based on a shift from hunting and gathering life to food producing and sedentary village life. Pottery too comes into use in this period, though aceramic (i.e., pre-pottery) Neolithic life is also noticed at certain places. The Neolithic phase did not start simultaneously in all parts of the country. Thus, whereas at Mehrgarh (Pakistan) its beginning goes back to the seventh millennium BC, in the Gangetic valley and other parts of inner India, it appears much later.

Northern Black Polished Ware (NBPW)

A distinctive pottery with highly lustrous polish, usually in black. It is a thin, well-fired and wheel-made pottery of well-levigated clay. Though distributed over a wide area extending up to Gujarat and the Deccan, it is found primarily in the mid-Gangetic Valley. It is dated between 600 BC – 200 BC and is associated with the growth of towns, trade and metallic currency in northern India in the sixth century BC.

Ochre Coloured Pottery (OCP)

It is a type of pottery found largely in western Uttar Pradesh (Upper Gangetic Valley) and is dated between 1800 BC – 1100 BC. It is wheel-made but has coarse fabric and is ill-fired. It has orange or dark red slip (coating) which on handling rubs off easily leaving an ochrous colour on fingers, and hence the name. The OCP layers have revealed the use of copper but not iron. It is thus associated with the Rig Vedic or Early Vedic period when, as it is normally presumed, people had no knowledge of iron.

Painted Grey Ware (PGW)

It is a pottery that is well-fired and is thin in form. It is distributed mainly in the Upper Gangetic region and is placed between 1100 BC – 600 BC. It is of grey colour and has paintings in linear and dotted patterns in black. It is associated with Later Vedic Culture and is marked by the beginning of the use of iron and the development of agricultural activities in northern India.

Palaeobotany

A field that investigates and analyses the botanical remains recovered from archeological remains.

Palaeolithic (literally, Old Stone Age)

It covers the largest period of human history extending from roughly 2 m.y.a. to 12000/10000 BP. It is marked by the evolution of human beings through various extinct species and their struggle for survival in hostile environment. It is divided, on the basis of growing tool technologies, into three sub-periods, viz., the Lower Palaeolithic, characterized by handaxes and chopper-chopping tools; the Middle Palaeolithic by medium sized flake tools; and Upper Palaeolithic by stone blade and bone tools. The Palaeolithic people lived in small groups termed as bands and their subsistence was based on hunting and gathering.

Pastoralism

A mode of subsistence based on rearing of livestock, usually cattle, sheep and goat. It involved a process of constant movement between two or more pasture areas. In extreme cases it may refer to a wholly nomadic life, but in some cases it may just be one feature of the agriculture- based sedentary life.

Palaeomagnetic Dating

A scientific dating technique based on the study of changes in the intensity of earth's magnetic field with time. These changes are noticed in different materials such as lava floors and lake sediments.

Pebble Tools

The earliest and the most primitive type of tools made by

striking off a few flakes from the edge of a pebble to produce an irregular working edge. By a process of gradual refinement these tools developed into hand-axes.

Pit Dwelling

It refers to the dwelling structures constructed by digging a pit in the ground and placing a thatched structure on top for protection from cold. To enter the pit, suspended ladders were used. Pit-dwellings were an important feature of the Neolithic Cultures of Kashmir.

Pleistocene

A geological period dated mainly between 2 million years ago to 12000/10000 BP. In this period, large part of the world was covered with ice-sheets. It is also the period when modern humans evolved progressively through many extinct species. It covers almost whole of the so-called Palaeolithic or Old Stone Age and ends with the final but gradual retreat of the ice-sheets.

Point

A tool of stone, bone or metal, having a sharp pointed end. It could be used as an arrowhead or some hole making device.

Pollen Analysis or Palynology

An analysis of fossil pollen as an aid to reconstruct past vegetation and climate.

Potassium-Argon (K-ar) dating

A scientific dating technique which is used in archaeology mostly for dating volcanic deposits with early hominid remains. It is based on the principle of recording the radioactive decay of K_{40} isotope of potassium. The half-life of

K_{40} is 1250 million years.

Post-Processual Archaeology

This term, coined by Ian Hoddar in 1986, encompasses within itself various approaches to archaeological studies including contextual archaeology, gender archaeology and cognitive archaeology.

Pottery

It is the most common find at any archaeological site. Its form, fabric and manufacturing techniques are used by archaeologists to explain the cultural variation or close relationship between different cultures. Pottery appear with the emergence of agriculture in the Neolithic period and was used not only for eating and drinking but also for storing cereals and liquids, and even for ceremonial purposes.

The primary raw material of pottery is clay which when mixed with water becomes elastic enough to be turned into a desired shape by hand or wheel. In the earliest stage, pottery was hand-made and crude. Small pots were made by pressing a lump of unbaked clay by hand. Storage vessels were made by making coils of clay and putting them one above the other. This ware is called "**coiled ware**" and was unbaked. It was only after the introduction of potter's wheel that significant advances were made in pottery making.

Clay for pottery is first dried, ground and sieved to remove impurities. The refined clay is mixed with water and made into a paste. The tempering material like wheat, rice husk, chopped grass and animal dung are mixed into the clay to prevent cracks and breakages. Sometimes unbaked vessels are placed on mat to prevent the bottom from sticking to the ground leaving in the process **mat impression** on the bottom.

Such impressions can be found on Neolithic pottery from Burzahom (Kashmir) and Chirand (Bihar). Sometimes storage vessels are beaten by wooden mallet (hammer) wrapped in a cord with support of stone from inside to enlarge the size of the pot before putting it on fire. Such **cord-marked pottery** is characteristic of Neolithic cultures of eastern and north-eastern India.

After making a vessel, a slip or coating is applied on the surface of a vessel to close the pores on the clay. Pots are also decorated before placing them in the kiln. Baking is done either in open kiln or closed kiln at varying degrees of temperature. When it is a closed kiln, smoke and gases do not escape and the pots turn grey or black. But when the smoke is allowed to escape, the pots turn red because of oxidization i.e., contact with oxygen in the air. Other colours like cream or buff depend upon the nature of the slip applied to the surface of the pot. When pots are made of thoroughly refined clay and are well fired, they are strong and sturdy.

There are large varieties of ceramics identified with various phases of human growth. Some of these such as OCP, PGW, NBPW are treated culture specific (see respective entries) while others like Black-and-Red Ware are found in many cultural areas and cover a long time span.

Prehistory

The term is used since nineteenth century to refer to the period of human history before writing was introduced. It broadly covers the time when modern man was evolving through various extinct species and was using stone tools and implements to feed and protect himself. Basically, it refers to a period of change in human subsistence pattern from hunting and gathering to the domestication of plants and animals.

Pressure Flaking

A technique of producing stone tools by applying pressure rather than a direct hit on to the edge of an object from which tools are detached. Pressure flaking requires a much greater degree of precision and makes it possible to detach regular or symmetrical and smaller flakes. This technique is indicative of well thought out planning and foresight on the part of early humans.

Processual Archaeology

Once called "New Archaeology," it is an approach to archaeological studies which formally began with the argument set forth by Kent Flannery in 1960s that "culture process" rather than "culture history" should be the true aim of archaeological research. It tends to seek help from other disciplines such as anthropology, ecology, sociology and other related subjects to analyse the factors underlying the growth of a particular culture rather than simply presenting archaeological data as self-evident.

Protohistory

A period that bridges the gulf between Prehistory, which is based on the interpretation of mute archaeological remains, and history when literary texts become the chief source of information. In Indian context, it normally covers a period from 3000 BC to 600 BC.

Radiocarbon Dating or C_{14} Dating

A method of measuring the age of a Prehistoric organic material (bone or wood) by estimating the decay of C_{14} in it. After a flaw was noticed in the earlier C_{14} dates, these have now been **calibrated** (corrected and adjusted) after revising the half-line of carbon to 5730 years. The **half-line** refers to the length of time taken by half of the radiocarbon atoms to decay, e.g., if there is 40 gram of carbon, 20 gram of its decay will represent 5730 years, and next half of it, i.e., 10 gram will constitute another 5730 years and so on.

Remote Sensing

A scientific device that is used to explore and identify ancient riverbeds (palaeochannels) and other features underlying the earth's surface with the help of images collected by LANDSAT [Land sat (ellite)], a satellite to obtain data on earth's natural resources], by using highly powerful sensors.

Rock Shelters

These are large cave-like natural structures formed by a normal process of weathering or erosion of sedimentary rocks which gradually come to rest on each other. The Vindhya hills of Madhya Pradesh contain many such shelters which were used by early humans for habitation as well as paintings.

Rouletted Ware

Pottery having dotted bands or stripes produced with the help of a rouletted or a toothed wheel. It is well-fired and has a fine fabric. It is distributed largely in south India but has also been found along the coast of West Bengal. Dated to early centuries of the Christian era, it was believed to be Mediterranean in origin but recent researches suggest it could be an Indian derivation.

Scraper

An implement of stone or bone or even metal having a specially prepared scraping edge that could be worked by the force of fingers. It is of many varieties such as convex, round or straight and could be used for scraping hides or smoothening wood.

Site

A place or an area where ancient artifacts are found by an archaeologist.

Seriation

A method of arranging artifacts or assemblages found in archaeological excavations into a sequence on the basis of their similarity in style, material and functional utility. First adopted by Christian Thomsen of Denmark in the 19th century, it is still used as a means of constructing relative chronology when there is a lack of clear stratification.

Settlement Archaeology

A branch of archaeological studies which aims to examine the remains of Prehistoric habitational sites in relation to their environment and resource areas. It is helpful in understanding the spatial patterning in a particular region.

Site-Catchment Analysis

It is a concept that focuses on the evaluation of natural resources (food as well as minerals) which lay within an easily exploitable distance of a given settlement to justify the presence of humans in that area. The term, coined by Eric Higgs in 1970, became an important method in the economic analysis of Prehistoric sites. The "catchment area" is defined as an area where resources could be available within a day's walk, say around ten km in the case of pre-agricultural communities. K. Paddayya used this technique in his analysis of Prehistoric sites in the Hunsgi valley, Karnataka.

Slip

It refers to a coating on pottery by a liquid clay or mud-fluid before firing. The function of slip is two-fold. Firstly, it helps in closing the pores in the clay, and secondly, it smoothens the surface of the vessels and makes them attractive. Slipped surface is offen burnished or polished by repeated rubbing with stone pebbles or some similar material.

Stratigraphy

A concept based on the law of superimposition, borrowed from Geology. It suggests that when a deposit overlies another, the upper must have accumulated later in time than the lower. It has been helpful in providing a relative chronological sequence of a succession of layers.

Terrace

Vast step-like features along a valley. These are usually caused by the receding of the stream which once flowed at a much higher level than at present. Since each terrace represents an earlier bottom of the stream, the top-most terrace is treated as the oldest in date, and accordingly the artifacts found there are considered to be the earliest.

Terracotta

The term refers to figurines or other objects made of baked clay. Terracotta objects, because of their inherent stability, are found in large numbers at the archaeological sites.

Three-Age System

A scheme dividing earliest phases of human history into three periods — Stone Age, Bronze Age and Iron Age. It was first formulated by Danish scholar, C. Thomsen in the nineteenth century as a means to classify the collection in the National

Museum of Denmark. These ages, he argued, must have followed each other. His view soon got confirmation from the material remains recovered in the archaeological excavations. But at the same time it also became apparent that these ages do not represent a unilinear development, and at many places stone tools continued to be used long after metal was introduced.

Tradition

In archaeological context, it is used to describe the continuity of similar technological style in the making of artifacts, whether stone tool or pottery. It is suggested that similarity in form and style indicates an underlying cultural connection or tradition.

Uranium-Series Dating or Th/U Dating

One of the many methods of scientific dating. It is based on the measurement of disequilibrium between the decay of two different types of uranium.

Use-Wear Analysis

The study of damage on a Prehistoric stone tool as a result of its utilization. The damage can be identified by focussing on the fractured edge or the effect on polish. This analysis, pioneered by the Russian scholar, Semenoy, is greatly helpful in understanding the job or the purpose which a particular tool was used for.

Zooarchaeology

A study and interpretation of animal remains recovered from the archaeological site. Other common term for it is faunal analysis.

Bibliography and References

Agrawal, [1982], *The Archaeology of India*, London.

———, [1999], 'Chalcolithic Cultures and Technology in India,' in G.C. Pande (ed.), *The Dawn of Indian Civilization*, Vol. I, Pt. I, Centre for Studies in Civilizations, New Delhi, pp. 465-491.

———, [2000]. *Ancient Metal Technology and Archaeology of South Asia: Pan-Asian Perspective*, New Delhi.

———, J.S. Kharakwal [2002], *South Asian Prehistory : A Multidisciplinary Study*, New Delhi.

Allchin, B. and R. Allchin, [1982], *The Rise of Civilization in India and Pakistan*, Cambridge.

———, and R. Allchin [1997], *Origins of Civilization: The Prehistory and Early Archaeology of South Asia*, New Delhi.

———, F.R. [1963], *Neolithic Cattle-keepers of South India : A study of the Deccan Ashmound*, Cambridge.

Banerjee, N.R. [1965], *The Iron Age in India*, Delhi.

Bednarik, R.G., [2002], 'The Development of Indian Rock Art Studies Since Independence,' in S. Settar and R. Korisetter (eds.), *Indian Archaeology in Retrospect, Prehistory*, Vol. I, New Delhi, pp. 353-375.

Bhattacharya, D.K. [1989], *An Outline of Indian Prehistory*, New Delhi.

Chakrabarti, D.K. [1988], *Theoretical Issues in Indian Archaeology*, New Delhi.

———, [1992], *The Early Use of Iron in India*, New Delhi.

———, [1999], *India, An Archaeological Study*, New Delhi.

———, [2003], *Archaeology in the Third World, A History of Indian Archaeology Since 1947*, New Delhi.

———, and N. Lahiri [1996], 'The Iron Age in India. The Beginning and Consequences,' in *Purātattava*, 24, pp. 12-32.

———, K.K. (ed.) [1984], *Rock Art of India*, New Delhi.

Chattopadhyaya, U.C. [1996], 'Settlement Pattern and Spatial Organization of Subsistence and Mortuary Practices in the Mesolithic Ganges Valley,' in *World Archaeology*, 27, pp. 461-76.

Childe, V.G. [1934], *New Light on the Most Ancient East*, London.

———, [1958], *The Prehistory of European Society*, Penguin.

Chitalwala, Y.M. [1985], 'Late Harappan Cultures,' in S.B. Deo and K. Paddayya (eds), *Recent Advances in Indian Archaeology*, Pune, pp. 57-64.

Clark, G. [1977], *Prehistoric Societies*, London.

Commiade, L.A. and M.C. Burkitt, [1930], 'Fresh Light on the Stone Ages in South-east India,' *Antiquity*, 4, pp. 327-39.

Dennell, R.W. *et al.* [1988], 'Early Tool-making in Asia: Two Million-year-old Artifacts from Northern Pakistan,' *Antiquity*, 62, pp. 98-106.

Deo, S.B. [1985], 'The Megaliths: Their Culture, Ecology, Economy and Technology,' in SB Deo and K. Paddayya (eds.), *Recent Advances in Indian Archeology*, Pune, pp. 89-99.

Deo, S.B. and K. Paddayya (eds.) [1985], *Recent Advances in Indian Prehistory*, Pune.

Deo, S.B. and Joglekar [1996], 'Satellite Remote Sensing in Archaeology,' *Man and Environment*, 21, pp. 59-70.

Dhavalikar, M.K. [1988], *First Farmers of the Deccan*, Pune.

———, M.K. [1997], *Indian Protohistory*, New Delhi.

———, M.K. [2002], 'Early Farming Culture of Central India. A Recent Perspective,' in S. Settar and R. Korisettar (eds.), *Indian Archaeology in* Retrospect, *Prehistory*, Vol. I, pp. 253-76.

———, M.K., H.D. Sankalia, *et al.* [1988], *Excavation at Inamgaon*, Pune.

Gordon, D.H. [1958], *The Prehistoric Background of Indian Culture*, Mumbai.

Ghosh, A.K. (ed.) [1989], *An Encyclopaedia of Indian Archaeology*, 2 vols, New Delhi.

Gururaja Rao, B.K. [1972], *The Megalithic Culture in South India*, Mysore.

Habib, Irfan [2001], *Prehistory*, Delhi.

Joshi, R.V. [1978], *Stone Age Culture of Central India*, Pune.

Kajale, M.D. [1991], 'Current Status of Indian Palaeobotany,' in Jane Renfrew (ed.), *New Light on Early Farming*, Edinburgh, pp. 155-89.

Kenoyer, J.M. [1983], 'An Upper Palaeolithic Shrine in India,' *Antiquity*, 57, pp. 88-94.

Kennedy, K.A.R. *et al* [1992], *Human Skeletal Remains from Mahadaha, A Gangetic Mesolithic Site*, Cornell University.

Korisettar, Ravi [2002], 'The Archaeology of South Asian Lower Palaeolithic : History and Current Status,' in S. Settar and R. Korisettar (eds), *Indian Archaeology in Retrospect*, Vol. I, New Delhi, pp 1-65.

———, R., Venkatasubbiah, Dorian Duller [2002], 'Brahmagiri and Beyond : The Archaeology of the Southern Neolithic,' in Settar and Korisettar (eds), *Indian Archaeology in Retrospect*, Vol. I, pp. 151-237.

Leshnik, L.S. [1974], *South Indian "Megalithic" Burials*, Wiesbaden.

Lukacs, J.R. [1992], 'Dental Anthropology of Mesolithic Hunter-gatherers,' *Man and Environment*, 17, pp. 42-55.

———, J.R. [1993], 'Mesolithic Subsistence in North India: Inference from Dental Attributes,' *Current Anthropology*, 34, pp. 745-65.

Mc-Intosh, J.R. [1985], 'Dating of the South Indian Megaliths,' in *South Asian Archaeology*, 1983, Naples, pp. 467-93.

Mathpal, Y. [1984], *The Prehistory Rock Art of Bhimbetka, Central India*, New Delhi.

Mishra, S. [1992], 'The Age of the Acheulean in India: New Evidence,' *Current Anthropology*, 33, pp. 325-28.

———, S. [1994], 'South Asian Lower Palaeolithic,' *Man and Environment*, 19, pp. 57-71.

Misra, V.D. [1999], 'A Brief Note on Indian Stone Archaeology,' in G.C. Pande (ed.), *The Dawn of Indian Civilization*, Vol. I, Pt.-I, New Delhi, pp. 129-38.

———, V.D. [1999], 'Agriculture, Domestication of Animals, Ceramic and Other Industries in Prehistoric India : Mesolithic and Neolithic,' in G.C. Pande (ed.), The Dawn of Indian Civilization, Vol. I, Pt.-I, New Delhi, pp. 233-66.

———, V.D. [2002], 'A Review of the Copper Hoards and the OCP Culture,' in Settar and Korisettar (eds.), *Indian Archaeology in Retrospect*, Vol. I, New Delhi, pp. 277-86.

———, V.N. [1989], 'Stone Age of India: An Ecological Perspective,' *Man and Environment*, 14, pp. 17-64.

———, V.N. [2002], 'The Mesolithic Age in India,' in Settar and Korisettar (eds.), *Indian Archaeology in Retrospect*, Vol. I, New Delhi, pp. 111-25.

Mohapatra, G.C. [1985], 'The Lower Palaeolithic in India,' in K.N. Dikshit (ed), *Archaeological Perspective of India Since Independence*, New Delhi, pp. 1-8.

——— [1990], 'Soanian-Acheulian Relationship,' *Bulletin of The Deccan College*, 49, pp. 251-60.

Moorti, U.S. [1994], *The Megalithic Culture of South India : Socio-Economic Perspectives*, Varanasi.

Murthy, M.L.K. [1985], 'Pre-Iron Age Agricultural Settlements in South India : An Ecological Perspective,' *Man and Environment*, 14, pp. 65-81.

Narasimhaiah, B. [1980], *Neolithic and Megalithic Culture in Tamil Nadu*, New Delhi.

Neumayer, E. [1993], *Lines on Stone: The Prehistoric Rock Art of India*, New Delhi.

Paddayya, K. [1982], *The Acheulean Culture of the Hunsgi Valley (Peninsular India): A Settlement ystem Perspective*, Pune.

———, K. [1994], 'Investigations of Man-Environment Relationships in Indian Archaeology: Some Theoretical Considerations,' *Man and Environment*, 19, pp. 1-28.

———, K. [2002] - 'The problem of Ashmounds of Southern Deccan in the Light of Recent Research,' in K. Paddayya (ed)., *Recent Studies in Indian Archaeology*, New Delhi, pp. 81-111.

———, K. [2002], 'A Review of Theoretical Perspectives in Indian Archaeology,' in Settar and Korisettar (eds.), *Indian Archaeology in Retrospect*, Vol. IV, New Delhi, pp. 117-58.

———, K. (ed.) [2002], *Recent Studies in Indian Archaeology*, New Delhi.

Pal, J.N. [1981], 'Upper Palaeolithic Cultures of the Mid-Son Valley,' *Puratattava*, 12, pp. 23-30.

———, J.N. [1994], 'Mesolithic Settlements in the Ganga Plain,' *Man and Environment*, 19, pp. 91-101.

———, J.N. [2002], 'The Mesolithic Phase in the Ganga Valley,' in K. Paddayya (ed.), *Recent Studies in Indian Archaeology*, New Delhi, pp. 60-80.

———, J.N. [2002], 'The Middle Palaeolithic Cultures of South Asia,' in Setter and Korisettar (eds.), *Indian Archaeology in Retrospect*, Vol. I, pp. 67- 83.

Panja, Sheena [2002], 'Research on the Deccan Chalcolithic,' in

Settar and Korisettar (eds.), *Indian Archaeology in Retrospect*, Vol. I, New Delhi, pp. 263-76.

Pant, Sushila [1999], 'Cave Paintings of Central India,' in G.C. Pande (ed.), *The Dawn of Indian Civilization*, Vol. I, Pt.-I, New Delhi, pp. 205-31.

Pappu, R.S. [2002], 'The Lower Palaeolithic Culture of India,' in K. Paddaya (ed.), *Recent Studies in Indian Archaeology*, New Delhi, pp. 17-59.

Possehl, G.L. and P.C. Rissman [1992], 'The Chronology of Prehistoric India, From Earliest Times to the Iron Age,' in R.W. Ehrich (ed.), *Chronologies in Old World Prehistory*, 2 Vols., Chicago.

Possehl, G.L. [1999], *Indus Age, The Beginnings*, Oxford, New Delhi.

Raju, D.R. and Venkantsubbaiah, [2002], 'The Archeology of the Upper Palaeolithic Phase in India,' in Settar and Korisettar (eds.), *Indian Archaeology in Retrospect*, Vol. I, New Delhi, pp 85-109.

Rami Reddy, V. [1990], 'Ashmounds in South India,' in A. Sundara (ed.), *Archaeology in Karnataka*, Mysore, pp. 85-99.

Renfrew, C. and P. Bahn [1991], *Archaeology — Theories, Methods and Practice*, London.

Sahu, B.P. [1988], *From Hunters to Breeders: Faunal Background of Early India*, New Delhi.

Settar, S. and Ravi Korisettar (eds.) [2002], *Indian Archaeology in Retrospect*, 4 Vols, New Delhi: ICHR Publication.

Sharma, D.P. [2002], *Newly Discovered Copper Hoard Weapons of South Asia*, New Delhi.

Sharma, G.R. *et al.* [1980], *Beginnings of Agriculture*, Allahabad.

Sharma, R.S. [1996], *The State and Varna Formation in the Mid-Ganga Plains: An Ethnoarchaeological View*, New Delhi.

———, [2005], *India's Ancient Past*, New Delhi.

Shaw, Ian and R. Jameson (eds.) [1999], *A Dictionary of Archaeology*, Oxford, U.K.

Shinde, V. [2002], 'Chalcolithic Phase in Western India (Including Central India and the Deccan Region),' in K. Paddayya (ed.), *Recent Studies in Indian Archaeology*, New Delhi, pp. 157-88.

Singh, Purushottam [2002], 'Neolithic Cultures of Northern and Eastern India,' in Settar and Korisettar (eds.), *Indian Archaeology in Retrospect*, Vol. I, New Delhi, pp. 127-50.

Sinha, B.P. (ed) [1969], *Potteries in Ancient India*, New Delhi.

Sinha, Prakash [1999], 'Prehistoric Tool Technology,' in G.C Pande (ed.), *The Dawn of Indian Civilization*, Vol. I, Pt.-I, New Delhi, pp. 139-73.

Sonakia, A. [1985], 'Skull Cap of an Early Man from the Narmada Valley,' *American Anthropologist*, 87, pp. 612 ff.

Sonawane, V.H. [2002], 'Rock Art of India,' in K. Paddayya (ed.), *Recent Studies in Indian Archaeology*, New Delhi, pp. 266-94.

Sonawane, V.H. and A. Majumdar [2002], 'Post-urban Harappan Culture in Punjab, Haryana and Uttar Pradesh,' in Settar and Korisettar (eds.), *Indian Archaeology in Retrospect*, Vol. I, New Delhi, pp. 240-52.

Soundara Rajan, K.V. [1985], 'Middle Palaeolithic in India,' in K.N. Dikshit (ed.), *Archaeological Perspective of India Since Independence*, New Delhi, pp. 9-14.

Subbarao, B. [1958], *The Personality of India*, Baroda.

Sundara, A. [1985], 'Cultural Ecology of the Neolithic in India,' in S.B. Deo and K. Paddayya (eds.), *Recent Advances in Indian Archaeology*, New Delhi, pp. 39-57.

Thakran, R.C. [2000], *Dynamics of Settlement Archaeology (Haryana)*, New Delhi.

Thapar, B.K. [1985], *Recent Archaeological Discoveries in India*, Paris.

———, B.K. [1985], - 'Fresh Light on the Neolithic Cultures of India,' in K.N. Dikshit (ed.), *Archaeological Perspective of India Since Independence*, New Delhi, pp. 37-43.

———, B.K. and A.K. Sharma [1994], *Indian Megaliths in Asian Context*, National Museum Institute, New Delhi.

Thomas, P.K. [1974], 'Zoological Evidence from Prehistoric India with Special Reference to Domestication,' *Bulletin of the Deccan College*, 34, pp. 195-10.

Tripathi, Vibha [2002], 'The Protohistorical Culture of the Ganga Valley,' in K. Paddayya (ed.), *Recent Studies in Indian Archaeology*, New Delhi, pp. 189-15.

———, Vibha [2002] - 'The Age of Iron in India : A Reappraisal,' in Settar and Korisettar (eds.), *Indian Archaeology in Retrospect*, Vol. I,, New Delhi, pp. 287-11.

Varma, R.K. [1985], 'The Mesolithic Culture of India,' in K.N. Dikshit (ed.), *Archaeological Perspective of India Since Independence*, New Delhi, pp. 27 ff.

Verma, A.K. [1988], *Neolithic Culture of Eastern India*, Delhi.

Vishnu-mitter and R. Savithri [1990], 'The Environment and Economy of the Neolithic Cultures of South India: Palaeobotanical Evidence,' in A. Sundara (ed.), *Archaeology in Karnataka*, pp. 100-12.

Vita-Finzi and E.S. Higgs [1970], 'Prehistoric Economy in the Mount Carmel Area of Palestine : Site Catchment Analysis,' *Proceedings of the Prehistoric Society*, 36, pp. 1-37.

Wakankar, V.S. and R.R.R. Brookes [1976], *Stone Age Paintings in India*, London.

Wheeler, R.E.M. [1948] - 'Brahmagiri and Chandravalli-1947: Megalithic and Other Cultures in Mysore State,' *Ancient India*, 4, pp. 180-310.

Index